World of Words
500

World of Words 500

Michael Roses

Definitions printed with kind permission of Macquarie Dictionary and John Wiley & Sons.

Copy editing by rEd aWry
redawry.com.au

Dedication

To my parents Michael John Lowry and Veronica Colleen Lowry.

My sincere thanks to my lifelong friend Mr. Gerard Overman of Perth, Western Australia for introducing me to the wonderful world of words, with his own profound mastery of significant words and to Ms. Enya Patricia Brennan and Mr. Tony O'Connor (deceased) for rekindling my ailing spirit during troubled times, with their enchanting music.

Words crystallise thoughts

Michael Roses 2016

Welcome to my wonderful world of words!

It is so true that words crystallise thoughts – the power intrinsic within words can encapsulate the notions that swirl within your mind into one neat little bundle that allows you to comprehend and understand your own thoughts and to then express yourself clearly.

World of Words 500 is undoubtedly one of the best selections of powerful words ever assembled and so by reading this book you will be elevated to the highest level of communication ability.

World of Words 500 is an ideal resource for any person hoping to excel in essay writing in high school or college or in pursuing any career in which communication is important.

You will surprise yourself how frequently you will use these 500 important words in your daily communication once you have read this book.

So please enjoy and tell your friends about my *World of Words 500* too.

Chapter 1

Abstain

1. to refrain voluntarily from, especially from drinking or enjoying something.

If you wish to be healthy, you should abstain from consuming too many animal fats in your food.
The contestants in the weight loss competition were required to abstain from consuming foods that contained an abundance of sugar.
The Republican members of Congress decided to abstain from endorsing the policies of their newly elected President.

Arduous

1. requiring great exertion; laborious; strenuous.

Walking from Perth to Kalgoorlie in Western Australia to search for gold in the 1890's, pushing a wheelbarrow containing your provisions, would have been an arduous exercise.
Climbing the difficult side of Mount Everest would be far more arduous than climbing the easy side.
The Egyptian slaves found construction of the pyramids to be an arduous task.

Benevolent

1. desiring to do good for others.

Isabella 1 was undoubtedly a benevolent Queen of Castile and Leon.
Former United States President Abraham Lincoln proved to be a President of profound benevolence in abolishing slavery.
Personal charity toward the feelings of others is a trait within benevolent minded people.

Forms of the word: benevolence

Conjunction

1. the act of conjoining; combination.

The air and sea search for the missing plane involved several countries working in conjunction with each other.
The Coast Guard worked in close conjunction with the police and the Marine Corps in responding to the massive damage caused by the hurricane named Katrina.
Fighting drug barons required law enforcement agencies to work in conjunction with local pimps.

Denounce

1. to condemn openly; assail with censure.

Libyan dictator Muammar Gaddafi decided to denounce terrorism so he could turn his attention to exacting his nation's wealth by graft.
Fundamentalist Christian churches denounce all other religious beliefs, out of gross ignorance.
Martin Luther denounced the practice of the Catholic Church of exacting monetary indulgences for the forgiveness of sin.

Forms of the word: denounced, denouncing, denouncement

Encompass

1. to form a circle about; encircle; surround.

The Indian warriors were so numerous they were able to encompass General George Custer and his troops.
The Bluefin tuna would completely encompass the school of sardines.

2. to enclose; contain

The Treasurer was asked whether the legislative changes would encompass any existing taxation legislation.

Expunge

1. to strike or blot out; erase; obliterate.

For the purpose of church unity, the Catholic Church decided to expunge a lot of decadent ritualism.
As he had been driving a sick person to the hospital emergency department, the taxi driver requested the magistrate to expunge his speeding fine.
It will be difficult to expunge racism from the broad community when so many of our politicians are blatantly racist.

Forms of the word: expunged, expunction

Folly

1. the state or quality of being foolish.

The concept of a space elevator to launch satellites into space seems to be folly considering it would need to be about eighty kilometres high.

2. a foolish action, practice, idea, etc.

He soon came to realise that his attempt to climb Mt. McKinley in Alaska without oxygen was absolute folly.
It was total folly to organise an ultra-marathon race in the heat of northern Australia.

Illicit

1. not permitted or authorised; unlicensed; unlawful.

Somehow illicit drugs always find their way into our maximum-security prisons.
They tried to use a hovercraft to deliver illicit drugs across the Everglades.
If the communists' bible – Karl Marx's *Das Kapital* – became an illicit item, it would probably be a good idea.

Inflict

1. to impose as something that must be borne.

Roman Emperors were particularly voracious in the way they would inflict exorbitant taxes upon the Jewish people.
No person has a right to inflict their extremist political or religious views upon others who lack the quality of discernment.
It is distinctly possible that the COVID-19 coronavirus has been inflicted upon humanity as a consequence of biological weapons manufacture.

Intuition

1. the direct perception of truths, facts etc., independently of any reasoning process.

The Apollo 13 astronauts had to use their intuition to return to Earth.
The early explorers had no maps but used their intuition to reach the river mouth.
Thomas Edison was able to invent so many new technologies with his intuition and by using problem solving techniques.

Forms of the word: intuitive

Microcosm

1. anything regarded as a world in miniature.

The first people to settle on Mars will need a huge dome to establish a microcosm of conditions on Earth.
The evolution of species in Madagascar represents a microcosm of the evolutionary path of all species.
The so-called Islamic State is a microcosm of ignorant, ill-informed and brainwashed people who don't know what cause they are fighting for.

Forms of the word: microcosmic

Ostracise

1. to exclude by general consent from society, privileges, etc.

If you deliberately ostracise people within your local church group, you will receive bad karma in return.
Good people will nurture friendships rather than ostracise someone who is a loner.
In ancient times lepers were ostracised as a means of disease control.

Forms of the word: ostracism

Portray

1. to represent by a drawing, painting, carving or the like.

There are so many examples of cave drawings that portray the arrival of aliens that we do need to consider whether our planet might have been visited for centuries.
The student compiled a composite map for her geography class to portray that the Amazon Basin is almost as large as Australia and the mainland United States.

2. to depict in words, describe graphically.

The history teacher endeavoured to portray what Marie Antoinette really meant about cakes.

Forms of the word: portrayal

Rampant

1. violent in action, spirit, opinion, etc.; raging; furious.

Army ants form a rampant destructive force when they decide to move.
Road rage is becoming so rampant because as populations grow our social bonds weaken.
Al Capone's men resorted to rampant violence that culminated in the Saint Valentine's Day massacre.

Relegate

1. to send to some lower position, place or condition.

Captain Kirk saved the planet Earth, but the Galactic Council still decided to relegate him from the rank of Admiral to the rank of Captain.
The Australian Football League decided to relegate the coach who had administered drugs to his players.
If we keep going the way that we are, we will relegate planet Earth to becoming a desolate rock similar to the planet Mercury.

Repugnant

1. distasteful or objectionable.

There are few things more repugnant than people who will take the lives of others, for love of money.
The Saint Valentine's Day Massacre was so repugnant that the United States Congress decided to end the prohibition of alcohol.
The oppression of African people by the former white government of South Africa was one of the most repugnant episodes in human history.

Reverberate

1. to re-echo or resound.

The impact of the melting of the Arctic Ice Sheet will reverberate around the entire globe.
The granting of land right to Australia's Aboriginal communities in Queensland will justifiably reverberate throughout the entire country.
The impact of the Beatles first appearance on the *Ed Sullivan Show* in February 1964 would reverberate through every form of youth culture.

Forms of the word: reverberation

Stultify

1. to make, or cause to appear, foolish or ridiculous.

It seems that all television networks endeavour to stultify Sarah Palin.
The television network compiled a dossier of George W. Bush's bloopers, in an attempt to stultify his reputation.
It is an intrinsic aspect of politics to use Parliament to stultify the opposition.

Surreal

1. of or relating to the dreamlike experiences.

The first images from the Hubble Telescope after the mirrors were rectified were so surreal that even the astronomers could not believe their eyes.
Canoeing in the waters of the Alaskan rivers is a totally surreal experience.
The plane ride from Queenstown to Milford Sound and its concomitant boat ride through the fiord is one of the most surreal experiences in this world.

Chapter 2

Adept

1. highly skilled; proficient; expert

Some accountants are adept at appraising business profitability, but most are not.
Navy pilots are extremely adept at landing their jet aircraft onto aircraft carriers.
Athletes involved in track and field events such as hurdles, high jump, javelin or pole vault, need to be absolutely adept at exercising their skills.

Forms of the word: adeptly, adeptness

Amicable

1. characterised by or exhibiting friendliness; friendly; peaceable.

If the aliens who arrive on planet Earth in their spaceships did not have a basic amicable nature, we would all be in a lot of trouble.
Relations between the United States and Japan have been peacefully amicable since WWII.
People who have an amicable personality generally establish and retain more lifelong friendships than people who do not have such a personality.

Bigot

1. a person who is intolerantly convinced of the rightness of a particular creed, opinion, practice, etc.

Only a bigot would denounce all other religious belief systems.
It was because he was a total bigot that the Pentecostal preacher told the Buddhists that they were destined to hell for eternity.

A new wave of bigoted people are protesting against the intake of refugees in many Free World countries.

Forms of the word: bigoted, bigotry

Connotation

1. that which is connoted; secondary implied or associated meanings.

She didn't actually say that she hated the winning Miss Universe, but there was a distinct connotation in her remark.
The Secretary of Defence warned the errant dictator with a remark that the dictator duly interpreted as a connotation of a possible military response.
The prosecuting attorney made a remark before the court that was a clear connotation to the defendant's previous convictions.

Criterion

1. a standard of judgment or criticism; an established rule or principle for testing anything.

An important criterion for success in business is to be diligent with book-keeping.
In enforcing the main criterion of strict self-control, the United States Navy selected the best candidates to be its elite Seals.
So many people volunteered to go to Mars that NASA had to revise its selection criteria.

Forms of the word: criteria

Deprecate

1. to express earnest disapproval of; urge reasons against; protest against (a scheme, purpose, etc.)

The Nixon Administration set out to deprecate the Chilean President Salvador Allende's plan to nationalise his nation's copper mines.
Virtually all nations openly deprecate the present-day government of North Korea for its rocket launches.
Environmentalists staunchly deprecate the further exploitation of fossil fuels with good reason.

Forms of the word: deprecated, deprecating, deprecation, deprecatory

Endemic

1. limited to a particular group or place, as a disease.

At the time of Jesus Christ, lepers contracted the disease that was endemic to the area.
The Tasmanian devils' facial tumour is a disease that is endemic to this species in Australia.
Tourists are contracting dengue fever in south-east Asia as the disease is endemic to tropical climates.

Extrapolate

1. to infer (what is not known) from that which is known; conjecture.

The sample was sufficiently large to allow the researchers to extrapolate their conclusions about Calicivirus to the entire population of rabbits.
The Bureau of Statistics will take a sample then extrapolate the results to the entire population.
The practice of the superannuation fund manager usurping funds from the woman's account for insurance costs, without her knowledge, could be extrapolated to the entire industry.

Forms of the word: extrapolated, extrapolating, extrapolation

Frantic

1. wild with excitement, passion, fear, pain, etc.; frenzied; characterised by or relating to frenzy.

The astronauts made a frantic effort to repair the spacecraft while they still had oxygen.
There were frantic scenes at the airport after the plane had crash-landed.
Certain East European Parliaments are characterised by some rather frantic fisticuffs.

Forms of the word: frantically

Initiate

1. to begin, set going, or originate.

It was undoubtedly Liverpool's Beatles who initiated the revolution in popular music.
The philanthropist decided to initiate a class action on behalf of retailers who were dispossessed by retail property developers.
The new Prime Minister sought to initiate a new thrust for innovative products and technologies.

Forms of the word: initiated, initiating, initiator

Juxtaposition

1. a placing close together.

Napoleon examined a juxtaposition of his forces against those of Prussia before he decided to do battle.

2. position side by side.

The business assessor devised a juxtaposition of this business against others in the same industry.

She pointed out to her drug dependent husband that her income, juxtaposed against his in recent years, showed she was carrying him as a passenger.

Nexus

1. a tie or link; a means of connection.

The nexus between the corrupt police and the prostitution racket was obvious.
There is now a clear nexus between the tax avoidance strategies of transnational corporations and the budget deficits of all western governments.
The business assessor pointed out the clear nexus in the trading statements to demonstrate that the fraudsters had transferred revenue between them.

Perpetrate

1. to perform, execute, or commit (a crime, deception, etc.).

The dictator decided to perpetrate gross atrocities against dissidents in an attempt to deter his rivals.
Terrorists are now inclined to perpetrate attacks against innocent civilians rather than military targets.
The axis of evil perpetrated the most horrific atrocities in the history of humanity, against the Jews and allied forces.

Precocious

1. forward in development, especially mental development, as a child.

Albert Einstein's primary school teachers regarded him as a rather precocious young man, but he was a lot smarter than them.

2. prematurely developed, as the mind, faculties, etc.

It was because of her husband's philandering that the princess made her decision to leave the precocious young prince.
In her rendition of Gigi, actress Audrey Hepburn was made out to be a rather precocious young lady.

Querulous

1. **full of complaints; complaining.**

The coach was always querulous at post-match media conferences because his team constantly lost.
To state that former United States President Donald Trump is an habitually querulous person would be a gross understatement.
Their father became a rather querulous man because his six teenage children were so lazy.

Remorse

1. **deep and painful regret for wrongdoing; compunction.**

The young murderers showed no remorse for their actions in slaying the jogger, who was completely unknown to them.
The former South African President announced his remorse for the incarceration of Nelson Mandela.
There is no doubt that terrorists will show no remorse for the carnage they cause.

Repulse

1. **to produce a feeling of strong aversion in; disgust.**

The actions of the terrorists who ran down and slayed Lee Rigby would repulse the entire world.

The Syrian government used deadly gas to murder thousands of its citizens in a campaign of terror that would repulse civilised nations.
The whole world has been repulsed by pervasive child abuse in a number of organizations endowed with the care of children.

Speculate

1. to think or reflect, especially with incomplete evidence; meditate or conjecture.

NASA launched the Kepler telescope but presently can only speculate about the possibility of life on exoplanets.
With the advancements in computer technology since the inception of the personal computer, we can only speculate about where the technology will take us at any point of time in the future.

2. to buy and sell goods, shares etc., in the hope in the hope of a profit or gain from a change in their market value.

The Wall Street stock market has stringent controls in place to deter those who might speculate with inside knowledge.

Subsume

1. to take up into or include in a larger or higher class or a more inclusive classification.

The hardware giant bought out its main competitor in an attempt to subsume all competition.
The grocery chains were rationalising for efficiency, but this meant the larger stores would subsume the smaller ones.
Hopefully, the move towards democracy in northern African states will subsume all autocratic dictatorships.

Tedious

1. marked by tedium; long and tiresome.

She found her job of filing deposit slips in the bank a totally tedious one.
Karl Marx thought the production line workers had a tedious job, but they enjoyed it because they didn't have to make decisions.
There is absolutely no doubt that machines and technology will continue to take over a lot of tedious tasks.

Chapter 3

Affront

1. a personally offensive act or word; an intentional slight; an open manifestation of disrespect; an insult to the face.

The British media regarded the former Australian Prime Minister who put his arm around the Queen to have perpetrated a serious affront.
The Malaysian Airlines considered suggestions of pilot sabotage as an affront to its professionalism.
Some questions that people ask regarding your personal life are a serious affront to your dignity.

Astute

1. of keen penetration or discernment; shrewd; cunning.

One needs to be an astute person to mix it with others within the rigors of the New York Stock Exchange.
Apple founder, Steve Jobs, was certainly an astute and dynamic innovator and businessman.
Many of our politicians are not particularly astute in anything.

Forms of the word: astuteness

Augment

1. to make larger, enlarge in size or length, increase

Once our robots initially establish a future colony on Mars, all stakeholders will need to cooperate to augment the provision of facilities for human habitation.
The Australian government funded the construction of the water pipeline from Lake Argyle in Western Australia to the Darling River catchment basin in

New South Wales, to augment the farming community's capacity to produce rice and fruit crops for export.
Sealed roads were constructed conjointly with the water pipeline from Lake Argyle to augment the mining industry's access to the expansive but undiscovered mineral resources in central Australia.

Cohort

1. any group or company.

The suicide bomber and his cohorts had been coerced by so-called clerics - who would never sacrifice their own lives.
As a cohort with her friends, she collected money for the Red Cross and the Catholic Missions.
The cohorts in crime had used gas to cause the teller machine to explode.

Conspicuous

1. easy to be seen.

Zebra have stripes to make themselves less conspicuous among the grasses of Africa, to lions.

2. readily attracting the attention.

It was her wedding day, but the bride was conspicuous by her absence.
There is no sense standing for a seat in Parliament if you are inconspicuous when it comes to kissing babies.

Deference

1. submission or yielding to the judgment, opinion, will, etc., of another.

It was out of deference to the Queen that the prince acceded to his son to become the next King of Lilliput.

2. respectful or courteous regard.

All Members of Parliament stood to pay deference to the deceased Senator.
It is out of deference to your own parents that you should honour your father and your mother.

Discrepancy

1. the state or quality of being discrepant; difference; inconsistency.

There could be a discrepancy between interpretations of the holy Quran, in relation to the notions of 'infidel' and 'jihad'.
There is an obvious discrepancy between the profits the transnational corporation had posted and the collective taxes it had paid to its host nations.
There is a slight discrepancy between the estimates of scientists who believe there are 200 billion stars in our Milky Way Galaxy and those who believe there are 300 billion.

Engender

1. to produce, cause, or give rise to.

The communications revolution will engender superior crop production for African farmers.
Modern technology ought to engender appropriate education levels for gifted students.
Future economic prosperity surely lies in engendering innovative ideas.

Extrinsic

1. extraneous; not inherent; unessential.

It seems that the needs of their electorates are somewhat extrinsic to many politicians' self-interest or to the interests of their political party.

2. being outside a thing; outward or external; operating or coming from without.

With so much conflict in the world today we wonder if violence is extrinsic to human nature or deep rooted within us.
Compassion for slaves was not extrinsic to the motives of former United States President Abraham Lincoln.

Generic

1. applicable or referring to all the members of a genus or class.

Enya's ethereal music cannot be classified as generic to any existing genre.
Homemakers save a lot of money when shopping by purchasing the generic brands of products.
Lions, tigers and leopards are all generic to the same class of big cats.

Implacable

1. not to be appeased or pacified; inexorable.

The independent Senator was such an implacable character in fighting for the poor that big money could not buy him out.
The Allies constituted an implacable fighting force during WWII.
The workers who initiated a class action to recover their superannuation funds were implacable before the courts.

Kowtow

1. to act in an obsequious manner; show servile deference.

Years ago, school children had to kowtow to all of their teachers.

The new Australian government would typically kowtow to the giant mining companies.
When in court one must be prepared to kowtow to the magistrate or judge.

Onerous

1. burdensome, oppressive, or troublesome.

Establishing a fully self-sufficient settlement on Mars could become an onerous building project.
Extracting the Taliban from the mountains of Afghanistan was an onerous task.
Constructing the Egyptian pyramids was not an onerous task for the aliens who built them.

Perplex

1. to cause to be puzzled over what is not understood or certain; bewilder; confuse mentally.

Most insurance companies will perplex consumers with legalistic fine print in their policies.
The Pakistani government withheld information about the whereabouts of Osama Bin Laden to perplex the search by the United States.
A lack of adequate instruction to new staff can be a totally perplexing experience for them.

Forms of the word: perplexed, perplexing

Predisposed

1. to give a previous inclination or tendency to.

The tsunami took so many lives because Pacific governments were so predisposed to complacency.
A fundamental tenet of the judiciary is to ensure that judges are not predisposed toward nor against the defendant.
Those who nominated candidates for the Academy Awards was blatantly predisposed against African American actors.

Recant

1. to withdraw or disavow (a statement, etc.), especially formally; retract.

The Catholic Pontiff literally had no choice but to recant his endorsement of the Cardinal as a character of impeccable repute.
The Alaskan Vice-President hopeful, Sarah Palin, was forced to recant her disparaging comment about Russia.
The Catholic concept of the "Anonymous Christian" - which implies that all good people, who are "Christ-like", will be received into heaven - has led many conservative Protestant churches to recant their more hardcore doctrine.

Rendition

1. a performance.

The Beatles rendition on the *Ed Sullivan Show* in February 1964 was a special moment in human history.

2. a translation.

The Pentecostal preacher's rendition regarding what Jesus meant by the words 'born again' was a classic example of dogmatic, exclusivist bigotry.

3. an interpretation, as of a role or a piece of music.

Matt Munro's rendition of "My Way" was definitely a superior version to that of Frank Sinatra – who seemed to talk his way through it.

Repute

1. regard in the view of others; reputation.

The longest serving monarch in human history, Queen Elizabeth II of England, was regarded by international leaders as a person of humble repute.
The leader of the Indonesian Mujahedeen Council, Abu Bakar Bashir, is considered by everybody in Australia as a person of ill repute.
To stand for a seat in Parliament, you must endeavour to be a person of honourable repute.

Subvert

1. to overthrow (something established or existing).

The International community must do everything possible to subvert organised terrorism.

2. to cause the downfall, or destruction of.

Australia's retail property developers use the cost of litigation to subvert independent professional property valuers.
The military regime in North Korea perpetuates its position of power by the total subversion of its people.

Forms of the word: subversion, subversive

Transcend

1. to go or be above or beyond (a limit, something with limits, etc.); surpass or exceed.

International sporting competitions do help us to transcend international conflict.
As a community we must transcend an historical tendency to neglect our remote indigenous communities.

When we do eventually colonise the Milky Way galaxy, we must transcend our tendency to create conflict.

Chapter 4

Ambience

1. environment; surrounding atmosphere.

The ambience within the United Nations Security Council meeting was sombre, as the Russian diplomat stood to deliver his rendition regarding the situation in the Crimea.
There was an ambience of anticipation as Enya took to the stage for her first live performance.
The ambience before the first bounce in the AFL Grand Final is electrifying.

Auspices

1. favouring influence; patronage.

Angola's refugees were provided with freshwater pumps under the auspices of the Catholic Mission.
The Sudanese farmers were provided with electric generators under the auspices of the Australian mining companies.
It is via the auspices of the annual Red Cross fundraising drive that so many homeless people are provided with basic shelter.

Forms of the word: auspicial

Compelling

1. **demanding attention or interest.**

There is compelling evidence that the Arctic Ice Sheet is melting at a rapid rate.

2. convincing.

American Bob Lazar has delivered some very compelling accounts of his experiences with reverse engineering alien space craft at location S4, south of Area 51.
The beacon left on the moon by the Apollo 11 astronauts that still sends signals back to planet Earth, is totally compelling evidence that the Apollo 11 mission actually did land on the moon.

Copious

1. large in quantity or number; abundant.

If the Arctic Ice Sheet does melt, there will not be a copious number of polar bears anywhere.
A modern-day economy utilises a copious amount of paper.
The English settlers brought just twenty-four rabbits to Australia but there are now copious numbers of rabbits everywhere.

Deficient

1. lacking some element or characteristic; defective.

A lot of highly skilled and experienced lawyers are deficient in grade-six arithmetic.

2. insufficient; inadequate.

There is a deficient supply of fresh water in most African countries.
Those aliens who turned up on Independence Day to destroy us were certainly deficient in compassion for people.

Forms of the word: deficiently

Disseminate

1. to scatter, as seed in sowing; spread abroad; diffuse; promulgate.

The televangelist used his television program to disseminate his voluminous books, tapes, CD's, DVD's, pamphlets, bangles, necklaces, bookmarks and anything else he could contrive to make a dollar.
Osama Bin Laden used various communication networks to disseminate his messages of belligerence and malice.
There is now an imperative need to disseminate information pertaining to electoral funding of our major political parties.

Forms of the word: disseminated, dissemination, disseminator

Equivocal

1. uncertain; not determined.

The assurances by the World Health Organisation that COVID-19 was not contrived in a laboratory were duly regarded by many governments as somewhat equivocal.

2. of doubtful character; questionable; dubious.

The Presidential candidate gave a rather equivocal commitment that he would never differentiate between people of differing religious persuasion.

3. having two or more meanings; ambiguous.

The pledge from Australia's banks that they would not pass on the costs of additional scrutiny to their customers, were less than unequivocal, by any interpretation.

Forms of the word: equivocally

Flout

1. to treat without respect; mock; scoff at.

When trekking in New Zealand, it is not a good idea to flout weather warnings.
If swimming in the Kakadu National Park, one should not flout warnings about the presence of crocodiles.
Arabian sheiks typically convey a facade of moral restraint within their own countries but flout such beliefs while visiting Western nations, flagrantly indulging in the consumption of alcohol and women.

Forms of the word: flouter, floutingly

Gumption

1. courage; resourcefulness.

The hairdresser showed quite some gumption by suing the retail developer for price fixing, with his extortionate rents.
In politics you must have sufficient gumption to level unsubstantiated accusations at the opposing parties.

2. practical common sense.

The astronauts displayed considerable gumption in deciding to abort their planned moon landing once they detected a problem with the electrical system.

Interject

1. to throw quickly between other things; to interpolate.

Former United States President Donald Trump had an idiosyncratic tendency to interject international dialogue with tweets, without due consultation with experienced diplomats.

2. to interrupt a conversation or speech; heckle.

The property developers' lawyers interjected the delivery by the state prosecutor at every stage during the trial.
It is a major affront to another person to interject while they are listening to somebody else on the telephone.

Forms of the word: interjection, interjector

Manipulate

1. to manage or influence by artful skill, or deviousness: to manipulate people; to manipulate prices.

The retail developers had put their heads together to manipulate the price of leasing space in their shopping centres.
Big business pours millions of dollars into the election coffers of conservative political parties, in order to manipulate the government's policies.
There is no doubt that transnational corporations manipulate international tax laws for considerable financial gain.

Forms of the word: manipulated, manipulating, manipulative, manipulator

Obfuscate

1. to confuse or stupefy.

Climate change deniers will resort to various assertions that lack scientific support to obfuscate the seriousness of this worldwide problem.
The official explanation of the debris at Roswell in 1947 as a weather balloon was a blatant obfuscation by the government to conceal the fact that intelligent aliens had arrived on planet Earth.

2. to darken or obscure.

The Government rejected the Opposition's proposal for a carbon tax as an obfuscation regarding the extent of the problem of global warming.

Forms of the word: obfuscated, obfuscating, obfuscation

Persevere

1. to persist in anything undertaken; maintain a purpose in spite of difficulty or obstacles; continue steadfastly.

The Democrats had lost office but decided to persevere with a carbon tax policy in order to cut greenhouse emissions.
To succeed as a triathlete, you must persevere until you are proficient at all three sports.
She wasn't attracted to him initially, but he did persevere and eventually she did bear his eight children.

Forms of the word: perseverance, persevered, persevering

Propound

1. to put forward for consideration, acceptance, or adoption.

In his response, the retail developer would propound his view that he had created a lot of jobs.
The property assessor addressed the court to propound his professional opinion that there would be many more jobs if retailers only had to pay true market value rents.
Donald Trump propounded his belief that he would not lose any votes if he shot somebody.

Reciprocal

1. given, felt, etc., by each to or towards each; mutual.

Our trade with China is a reciprocal arrangement - they buy our iron ore and we buy their “everything they make”.

The exchange of political prisoners was a reciprocal arrangement between the United States and Russia.
The Hindu concept of reincarnation involves a succession of incarnations based on reciprocal relationships, depending on whether you live life as a good person or as a bad person.

Forms of the word: reciprocally

Renounce

1. to give up or put aside voluntarily.

The Prince of Lilliput did decide to renounce his right to the throne in view of public perceptions.
The Catholic Church finally saw the light and decided to renounce the Rosary in favour of The Lord's Prayer - as Jesus had said.
The Australian Republican Party issued a proclamation before Parliament to renounce any allegiance to the King.

Forms of the word: renounced, renouncing, renouncement

Restitution

1. reparation made by giving an equivalent or compensation for loss, damage, or injury caused; indemnification.

Following the decisions from the High Court the governments of New Zealand and Australia were ordered to make restitution payments to their indigenous people.
After the war, the allies inflicted harsh forms of restitution payments upon the aggressor nations.
The property developer was ordered by the court to make restitution to all tenants who had been defrauded.

Stifle

1. to keep back or repress.

Failure to drink sufficient milk as a child will stifle the growth rate of your bones.
The levying of a flat company tax rate rather than a progressive rate does stifle fledgling businesses.
There is now a major international drive to stifle the radicalisation of youth.

Forms of the word: stifled, stifling

Succinct

1. expressed in few words; concise; terse.

She was not promoted because her responses in the interview were rather succinct when they really wanted her to elucidate.
He proposed to the supermodel but her one-word response – “no” - was rather succinct.
You might be a succinct communicator yourself, but some people do talk far too much.

Forms of the word: succinctly, succinctness

Ubiquitous

1. Ubiquity = the state or capacity of being everywhere at the same time; omnipresence.

We must ensure the ubiquitous Aussie bush fly does not hitch a free ride to Mars when we go there.
Despite the ubiquitous presence of galaxies in the universe, will there ever be enough resources for mankind?
When the Kiwi astronaut went to Mars, he did take along New Zealand's notoriously ubiquitous sand fly.

Chapter 5

Amiable

1. having or showing agreeable personal qualities, as sweetness of temper, kind-heartedness, etc.

Most Hindu and Buddhist people are very amiable people as their religious belief system teaches no malice toward others.
People who are amiable tend to have far more friends than people who are not.
Apart from their good looks and their revolutionary music, the Beatles enamoured everybody they met and the entire world with their amiable characters.

Authentic

1. entitled to acceptance or belief; reliable; trustworthy.

One day science might actually prove the Holy Shroud of Turin to be the authentic garment in which Jesus was buried.
The cave paintings portraying a spaceship landing on the pyramid proved to be authentic.
Despite his constant denials the adverse drug test results of the champion cyclist were, in fact, authentic.

Condescend

1. to behave as if one is conscious of descending from a superior position, rank, or dignity.

The chanteuse was visiting impoverished neighbourhoods in the Bronx, but it was clear she felt she had to condescend to talk to the local residents.

The Minister for Aboriginal Affairs went to the remote community of Jigalong, but it was obvious he felt he had to condescend when meeting their elders.
It is normal to perceive the King of England's feelings of condescension when he greets you - but he is up there.

Correlate

1. to place in or bring into mutual or reciprocal relation; establish in orderly connection.

Prudent financial management within the home requires a parent to correlate their total family income against their expenses.
The post-graduate researcher went to various supermarkets within the city to correlate their retail prices against average household income.
The legal case was determined by virtue of correlations between the plaintiff's and the defendant's expense accounts.

Forms of the word: correlated, correlating

Delve

1. to carry on intensive or thorough research for information, etc.

As a parent one should not delve too deeply into the affairs of one's children once they reach adulthood.
Be cautious if you decide to delve into gambling syndicates.
Scientists have decided to attach a two millimetre microchip to Tasmanian bees to delve into their movements.

Forms of the word: delved, delving

Embellish

1. to beautify by or as by ornamentation; ornament; adorn.

Enya set out to embellish her newly renovated Manderley Castle with marble walls - and her twenty-seven cats.

2. to enhance (a statement or narrative) with fictitious additions; embroider.

The students really did need a good vocabulary in order to embellish their writings.
During the Spanish Inquisition, it was common practice for accusers to embellish their testimony against the accused, with blatant untruth.

Forms of the word: embellisher

Esoteric

1. understood by or meant for a select few.

Successive United States Presidents have been instructed by alien visitors to remain esoteric regarding the aliens' presence here on Earth.

2. private; secret; confidential.

The United States Central Intelligence Agency requires its agents to be somewhat esoteric about their work.

3. (of philosophical doctrine, etc.) intended to be communicated only to the initiated.

There is no doubt that the Freemasons are an esoteric bunch of guys.

Fluctuate

1. to change continually, from one course, position, condition, amount, etc., to another.

The temperature will fluctuate a lot on Mars, but that Aussie bush fly will survive, don't worry!
Do not step outside your spaceship hoping for the temperature to fluctuate because it will always be absolute zero.
If you continue to gamble at the casino, your fortunes will fluctuate but eventually you will lose.

Forms of the word: fluctuated, fluctuating, fluctuation

Intervene

1. to come between in action; intercede.

Fortunately, the United States eventually decided to intervene in WWII and send copious amounts of military supplies to Britain.

2. to come or be between, as in place, time, or a series.

With so many different sports now able to hold their own world tournaments every four years and intervene between the Olympic Games and the FIFA World Cup, life should never be boring.

3. to fall or happen.

WWII intervened between the staging of the Olympic Games that were due to be held in 1940 and 1944.

Forms of the word: intervened, intervening

Mendacious

1. lying or untruthful.

People who steal are typically mendacious when it comes to testifying before the courts.
The former football legend was totally mendacious in giving his testimony regarding the death of his wife.

Most lawyers have no compunction about suggesting that their client resorts to blatant and flagrant mendacity before the courts.

Forms of the word: mendacity

Nullify

1. to make ineffective, futile, or of no consequence.

Almost every nation imposed a social distancing requirement upon its citizens in an attempt to nullify the contagious virus.
To become a compulsive gambler could nullify all of your years of hard-won savings very quickly.

2. to render or declare legally void or inoperative.

The world's Islamic leaders need to enter into dialogue with each other and denounce the perpetration of violence under the concept of "Jihad", to nullify false interpretations of the holy Quran by extremist fringe terrorist groups.

Peruse

1. to read through, as with thoroughness or care.

Before signing a commercial lease to rent retail space, ensure you have a lawyer peruse the document first.

2. to read in a leisurely fashion, with little attention to detail.

If you merely peruse your school textbooks rather than fully comprehending the contents you might not do as well in exams.
The antiques dealer in Bethlehem who was the first person to peruse the Dead Sea Scrolls, but decided they were worthless, had done so in a very cursory manner.

Qualm

1. an uneasy feeling or a pang of conscience as to conduct.

The judge had no qualm about sentencing the Boston bomber to life in prison without any prospect of parole.

2. a sudden misgiving, or feeling of apprehensive uneasiness.

Perhaps we should experience some qualms about bringing back the dinosaurs.
Prior to committing resources to assist Britain and France in World War II against the German aggressor, the people of the United States of America might have experienced a slight qualm about losing their sons in somebody else's war.

Recriminate

1. to bring a countercharge against an accuser.

The bomber tried to recriminate all non-religious people by branding them as being infidel.
In his testimony into his financial affairs the multi-millionaire shylock tried to recriminate his investors for trusting him.
The bikies who were on trial for drug running endeavoured to recriminate their former member, who had turned "dog", by claiming that he was the instigator of the plan to weld metal containers containing drugs within the hulls of ships.

Relent

1. to soften in feeling, temper or determination; become more mild or forgiving.

The international community will not relent in its determination to completely eradicate this heinous coronavirus.

Elon Musk's Space X program will never relent in attempting to establish a human colony on Mars, because it is inevitable that we will destroy this planet Earth.
Australia's jack jumper ants just won't relent in trying to jump onto your leg to deliver a nasty sting.

Replenish

1. to bring back to a state of fullness or completeness, as by supplying what is lacking.

Now that we have ransacked the planet Earth, perhaps we can start to replenish all areas that we have desecrated.
By constructing artificial reefs and recycling our food wastes into fish pellets we could replenish our stocks of ocean fish.
The Indonesian foresters were ordered to replenish all felled areas in order to arrest the problem of global warming.

Retribution

1. repayment for one's actions, especially evil.

The allied forces sought retribution for war crimes against the perpetrators of genocide, at the Nuremburg trials.
The people of Iraq felt no qualms about seeking retribution against Saddam Hussein for his torture and murder of thousands of innocent people.
The almighty deity who created the universe will exact retribution upon all wrongdoers.

Stigma

1. a mark of disgrace; a stain, as on one's reputation.

There should never be any feelings of stigma about being unemployed because today's workforce is such a dynamically changing place.
Ex-prisoners need a chance to integrate back into society without any stigma associated with their prior offences.
Most people who are declared bankrupt will feel some sense of stigma despite their plight being caused by others.

Superficial

1. shallow; not profound or thorough.

The church's handling of accusations made decades ago was an entirely superficial response.
The response of the actress to footage of starving children, that she "wouldn't mind being that thin but she wouldn't want all those flies and stuff" was aptly described by one commentator as superficial.
Okay, the farmer might need a wife to love him and care for him, to cook meals and shear the sheep, but all this talk of marriage within a few days of meeting is entirely superficial.

Vague

1. not definite in statement or meaning; not explicit or precise: vague promises.

It's best to be vague about your finances if confronted by a pesky, persistent and assertive financial planner.
The transnational internet provider proved to be quite vague when required to disclose international banking arrangements.

2. of an indefinite or indistinct character, as ideas, feelings, etc.

The young seminarian was very enthusiastic about the priesthood when he entered the seminary just three years earlier, but having mingled a little with some young nuns, he now felt rather vague about continuing.

Chapter 6

Averse

1. not willing; disinclined; reluctant; opposed (to).

There is no sense in joining the greenies if you have an aversion to kissing trees.
The helicopter pilot had his licence revoked because, as a greenie, it seemed that he was not averse to flying too low above the tall Karri trees near Pemberton in Western Australia.
As good people we must not be averse to providing aid to underdeveloped nations.

Forms of the word: aversion

Blasé

1. indifferent to and bored by the pleasures of life.

The petrol station attendant was completely blasé about his habit of smoking cigarettes whilst filling cars with petrol.
One ought not to be blasé about traversing New Zealand's alpine tracks without adequate protection from a sudden deluge.
We see the sky, the clouds, the stars, the trees and the oceans but are we sometimes blasé to the beauty of God's creation?

Circumspect

1. watchful on all sides; cautious; prudent.

All nations now need to be circumspect about burning fossil fuels.
It is advisable to be extremely circumspect about exclusion clauses if applying for income protection insurance.

The world's nations need to be circumspect when dealing with renegade states such as North Korea and Syria.

Forms of the word: circumspection

Clarify

1. to make or become understandable.

In order to achieve an efficient working environment, you may have to clarify the respective roles of the staff.
If you do not understand the exact implications of the mortgage documents the bank has asked you to sign, you should have a lawyer clarify them for you.
Counsellors will clarify comments from their clients as a form of feeding the client's own feelings back to them.

Forms of the word: clarification, clarified, clarifying, clarity

Conceptualise

1. to form an idea or ideas of.

On receiving images from the Hubble Deep Space Field, NASA scientists had difficulty conceptualising how anything could be as vast as the observable universe.
In order to start a new business, it may be necessary to conceptualise just how you will overcome the adversity you will experience.
The police could not conceptualise how a psychic person could provide so much accurate intricate detail about the murder case.

Forms of the word: conceptual, conceptualised, conceptualising

Concerted

1. arranged by agreement; prearranged; planned.

The insidious nature of racism is such that only a constantly concerted effort from both sides of the political spectrum is going to keep it in check.
The surf patrols from adjoining beaches were extending their areas of inspection in a concerted campaign to prevent body boarders from getting into difficulty.
The Australian kelpie and his master will conduct a concerted effort to round up those stupid sheep.

Confide

1. to show trust by telling secrets, personal matters, etc.

Your best friends are people that you can tell your most intimate secrets to and share your most personal feelings with, because you just know that you can confide in them, without being betrayed.
Some people cannot be trusted keeping intimate secrets to themselves, so be very discreet about in whom it is that you confide.

2. to entrust to the care, knowledge or good faith of another person.

The wayward prince sought a new concubine in whom he could confide.

Forms of the word: confidant, confided, confiding

Deceive

1. to mislead by a false appearance or statement; delude.

Never, ever, sign a document unless you carefully peruse it first to ensure somebody is not trying to deceive you.
The dictator claimed to have no weapons of mass destruction, but he was known to be totally deceitful in all things.

If you deceive your own spouse, you might find yourself sleeping on the couch for a period of time.

Forms of the word: deceit, deceitful, deceitfulness, deceived, deceiving, deception

Defy

1. to show no fear or respect for; resist boldly or openly.

If you are going to defy your employer's instructions not to drink and drive, you might anticipate a period of unemployment.

2. to provide a good defence against.

The British pilots in their Supermarine Spitfires and Hawker Hurricanes were able to defy the Luftwaffe's incursion into England.

3. to dare (someone) to do something thought to be impossible.

His wife's captious, carping criticisms of his reluctance to mow the lawn were so overbearing that he defied *her* to mow the lawn.

Forms of the word: defiance, defiant, defiantly, defied, defying

Deprive

1. to take away something possessed or enjoyed; dispossess; strip; bereave.

European settlement in Australia in the eighteenth century would deprive hundreds of communities of indigenous people of the land they needed to maintain a functional society.

2. to keep (a person, etc.) from possessing or enjoying something withheld.

When the time comes, hopefully aliens will not deprive we Earthlings of the right to establish a contingency colony on Mars.
The government of North Korea deprives its people of virtually all internationally sanctioned rights.

Forms of the word: deprived, depriving, deprivation

Dubious

1. **doubtful; uncertain.**

The claim by hard line fundamentalist religious groups that God made the world about seven thousand years ago, would seem dubious in the light of modern scientific knowledge.
Former U.S. President Donald Trump's claim that Australia's restrictive gun laws had led to a higher incidence of rape, was dubious to state the least.

2. **of doubtful quality; questionable.**

Somebody is already selling plots of land on Mars, but the authenticity of the title may be rather dubious.

Forms of the word: dubiousness

Endorse

1. **to give support to; approve.**

The environmentalists decided to endorse the candidate who vowed to stop wood chipping completely.
The United States Republican Presidential candidate was such a blatantly egotistical maniac, that even elder Republican statesmen refused to endorse him as their preferred Presidential nomination.
All nations signed the agreement to endorse the new protocol on climate change.

Forms of the word: endorsed, endorsement, endorser, endorsing

Enthral

1. **to hold the whole attention of; enchant.**

You will be totally enthralled by the scenery should you take a flight from Queenstown to Milford Sound in New Zealand.
When you arrive in Queenstown, New Zealand, make sure that you venture to the top of the gondola, because what you will see from there, of Lake Wakatipu and the surrounding mountains including The Remarkables, will enthral you.
Those first images from the Hubble Deep Space Field view were totally enthralling.

Forms of the word: enthralled, enthralling

Incite

1. **to urge on; stimulate or prompt to action.**

The worst thing you could do whilst in Africa is to incite the wildlife into a frenzy.
Some kids steal cars and drive dangerously through the streets in an attempt to incite the police into a chase.
Indonesia's number one terrorist, Abu Bakar Bashir, did his best to incite the Bali bombers into implementing their act of terror.

Forms of the word: incited, inciting, incitement

Inundate

1. **to overspread with or as with a flood; flood; deluge; overwhelm.**

If we do not restore the rabbit proof fence immediately, bunnies will inundate our farmlands.
Their tent on the banks of the Rees-Dart River near Queenstown became inundated with sandflies.
If we do allow the Aussie bushfly to hitch a ride to Mars, the planet would soon be inundated with them.

Forms of the word: inundated, inundating, inundation

Pacify

1. to bring into a state of peace, calm.

You may need to pacify the lady at the dog beach if your big dog starts a fight with her little dog.
The government's pledge to foster new industries in the towns affected by the new forest strategy was a clear attempt to pacify the people whose lives would be gravely disrupted.
The offer by Marie Antoinette to allow the peasants to eat cake was an attempt to pacify them, because they had no bread.

Forms of the word: pacifiable, pacified, pacifist, pacifying

Prominent

1. standing out so as to be easily seen; conspicuous.

The Grand Canyon is the most prominent land feature on our planet when viewed from the moon - and Olympus Mons is the most prominent landmark on the planet Mars.

2. standing out beyond a surface or line; projecting.

Perpendicular Point, just north of Greymouth on New Zealand's west coast, is one of the more prominent landmarks on this most remarkable stretch of coastline.

3. important; leading; well known.

The development of the canola crop, which has provided additional income to farmers as well as rejuvenating the soil, is one of the most prominent examples of how agricultural science can lead to multiple problem solving.

Quandary

1. a condition of not knowing what to do; dilemma.

You may find yourself in a quandary if you fall in love with two people at the same time.
She had saved well for her backpacking holiday, but her quandary was whether to go to New Zealand or to Europe.
Sir Winston Churchill could not understand President Roosevelt's quandary regarding a commitment to the war effort.

Spite

1. a keen, ill-natured desire to humiliate, annoy, or hurt another; venomous ill will (noun).

It is mainly out of spite that brainwashed, radical, political terrorists seek to disrupt peace-loving nations and rationalise their terrorist activities with exhortations to religious beliefs.

2. (in spite of) in disregard or defiance of; notwithstanding (noun).

NASA decided to launch the Hubble and James Webb Telescopes in spite of the cost - but thank God it did.

3. to direct one's spite or evil intention on (verb).

Terrorists will always be inclined to spite westerners because we live a life of comparative freedom.

4. to annoy, out of spite (verb).

One should not cut off one's nose to spite one's own face.

Forms of the word: spited, spiteful, spitefully, spiting

Terse

1. impolitely brief or bad-tempered, especially in one's speech.

The Apollo astronauts were understandably terse in responding to nitwits who put forth conspiracy theories, considering that the astronauts had returned moon rocks to Earth.
Pope Francis received a terse response from his College of Cardinals by intimating that the Catholic Church might relent on its hard-line doctrine pertaining to de facto marriages.
The police justifiably spoke quite tersely to the hoon who had just gone through a red traffic light and caused an horrific accident.

Forms of the word: terser, tersest

Chapter 7

Abrupt

1. sudden; without warning.

The battle of Little Bighorn came to an abrupt end because Custer's men were completely outnumbered.
NASA quite abruptly placed all lunar excursions on hold after aliens were found to inhabit the dark side of the moon.

2. brief and impolite in speech or manner; brusque.

The police officer had already had a gutful of abuse from drunk drivers when he spoke to the intoxicated woman quite abruptly.

Forms of the word: abruptly, abruptness

Affable

1. easy to talk to or to approach; polite; friendly.

The psychic woman was a truly affable character, but both her gift and her personality were based on her love for all people.
In the marriage stakes there is clearly a positive correlation between success and people who are affable rather than arrogant.
The Beatles impressed everybody in New York with their totally affable manner.

Forms of the word: affability, affableness, affably

Agitate

1. to excite; disturb; perturb.

It would not be wise to agitate an African bull elephant if you are a long way from your vehicle.
Perhaps one of the most important indicators of successful marriage is that at least one person in the relationship is prepared to pacify rather than to agitate their partner.

2. to try to get public support for something.

The forestry industry workers who were about to be displaced by the government's accord on logging on New Zealand's South Island were agitating for an amnesty period.

Forms of the word: agitated, agitating, agitation, agitative, agitator

Blatant

1. intentionally obvious or undisguised.

The hoons drove away from the petrol station so quickly without paying for their fuel that it was obviously a blatant theft.
The grass roots drug traffickers were blatantly distributing in the wee hours of the morning – house hopping by catching a taxi or an Uber ride.
There is a blatant lack of law enforcement against our banks and insurance companies for their contemptuous treatment of customers.

Forms of the word: blatantly

Brazen

1. shameless or cheeky.

Those brazen hoons swore at the police who stopped them for speeding.
The grey gulls of Antarctica will brazenly rob their neighbours' nests of materials, to construct their own nests.
African hyena will brazenly endeavour to force lions away from a carcass.

Forms of the word: brazenness

Comprise

1. to include, contain.

The writings of the great Chinese philosopher, Confucius, who advocated the great universal law of "do unto others as you would have them do unto you", comprise a set of values that would nurture social cooperation and harmony.

2. to be made up of; be composed of.

All of the stars we can see with the naked eye, plus hundreds of billions more, comprise the Milky Way Galaxy.
There are presently thirty franchised member clubs that comprise the United States National Basketball Association.

Forms of the word: comprised, comprising, comprisal

Confound

1. to mix so that the elements cannot be separated.

Debate in the historically significant referendum to recognise Australia's Aboriginal people in the nation's constitution was confounded by the conservative Liberal Party's typical strategy of creating fear and confusion.

2. to treat or regard mistakenly as the same; confuse.

Terrorist leaders will typically confuse gullible followers by confounding western affluent lifestyles with a supposed dearth of spiritual values.

3. to surprise or perplex.

The defence lawyer's line of complex questioning was a blatant attempt to confound the plaintiff.

Forms of the word: confounded

Conjure

1. to call upon or command by a spell, etc.

Why is it that so many people allow the tangential ideas of a cultist idiot – such as with the Jonestown, Heaven's Gate and Branch Davidian tragedies - to conjure images of immortality within their minds?
The opposition of criminal lawyers to mandatory sentencing was perceived by the judge as an attempt to conjure a similitude of justice when it was really to foster their own career prospects.
The discovery of so many exoplanets by NASA's Kepler telescope has conjured visions of we human beings colonising the galaxy.

Forms of the word: conjured, conjuring

Contempt

1. the condition of being despised; dishonour; disgrace.

Some people are just so blatantly racist that they deserve all of the contempt with which we can regard them.

2. the feeling with which one regards anything considered mean, vile, or worthless.

Historical records undeniably reveal that African slaves were treated with contempt by wealthy landowners in the decades prior to the American Civil War.

3. open disrespect of rules or orders of a court of law.

If you treat the process of law in the courts with contempt you can expect to spend some time in prison.

Forms of the word: contemptible, contemptuous

Deduce

1. to reach (a conclusion) from known or supposed facts; infer by logical reasoning.

There are so many dinosaur fossils in different levels of sedimentary rock that it is possible to deduce the age of the fossils.
From Max Weber's classical exposition *The Protestant Ethic and the Spirit of Capitalism* we can deduce why Protestants are generally wealthier than Catholics – they tend to work longer hours rather than to make more babies.
The James Webb Space Telescope will deduce whether there are galaxies beyond the most distant presently known.

Forms of the word: deduced, deducing, deducible, deduction, deductive

Derive

1. to receive, obtain, take, or trace (something) from a source or origin.

You know you are getting older when you derive more satisfaction from listening to the very beautiful Marilla Ness singing "Be Still for the Presence of the Lord" on Youtube, than you do by watching Mick Jagger and his Rolling Stones singing their rendition of "Satisfaction".
Modern day western governments could derive sufficient revenue to address their rising deficits by levying a wealth tax on all of the corporate moguls who have evaded or avoided tax through offshore tax havens.
It is surely miraculous how the tallest trees begin life as a tiny seed then grow to mighty heights by deriving nutrients from the ground.

Forms of the word: derived, deriving

Destitute

1. without the necessary things of life.

With so much wealth in the world, why are there still so many destitute children starving in Africa?
The decrepit old man in the worn pin stripe suit reeked of alcohol and nicotine and was obviously in a destitute state.
The tornados had wreaked so much havoc in the mid-west that thousands of people were left in a completely destitute situation.

Forms of the word: destitution

Emphatic

1. uttered, or to be uttered, with emphasis; strongly expressive.

The entire climbing party would have perished in the enormous landslide on Mt. Cook if their guide had not been so emphatic that a landslide looked imminent.

2. using emphasis in speech or action.

The farming lobby continued to be emphatically against daylight saving because of the effect it had on their cows - and those stupid sheep!

3. forcibly significant; strongly marked; striking.

The outcome of the referendum was an emphatic rejection of the proposal for daylight saving.

Forms of the word: emphatically

Exacerbate

1. to increase the strength or violence of (disease, ill feelings, etc.); aggravate.

If you respond to your neighbour's outburst about your loud music by turning the volume up, you will exacerbate his anger.

If your tent is covered in large sergeant bull ants (*Myrmecia*) somewhere near Mukinbudin while you are sleeping, stirring up their nest will only exacerbate your problem.
Dogmatic Pentecostal preachers who denigrate all non-Christians will only exacerbate the problem of terrorism that we see in the world today.

Forms of the word: exacerbated, exacerbating, exacerbation

Impose

1. to lay on or set as something to be paid, put up with, obeyed, fulfilled, etc.

If aliens are occupying the dark side of the moon, perhaps we should stay away but impose a tariff upon them.

2. to push or force oneself upon others.

You should not impose your will to attend a New Year's Eve party upon a person who likes to stay home and sleep.

3. to pass off dishonestly or deceptively.

If you stop at the cafe at New Zealand's Fox Glacier and impose yourself upon the outdoor seating reserved for people from the other tourist bus, you might find yourself in Picton while your luggage goes to Te Anau.

Forms of the word: imposed, imposing, imposition

Ludicrous

1. so stupid as to cause laughter; ridiculous.

The belief of fundamentalists that the world was created seven thousand years ago is regarded by intelligent, well educated people as entirely ludicrous.

The assertion that socialism is the answer to the world's economic ills has now been adequately exposed by the incompetence of the collective as absolutely ludicrous.
It is so ludicrous that a candidate who makes so many gaffes could be running for the Presidency of the United States.

Notorious

1. widely but unfavourably known.

The Indonesian fires had once again been started by wealthy transnational corporations with a notorious record in environmental vandalism.

2. publicly or generally known.

New Zealand's possums and Australia's rabbits are both notorious for running beneath your car if you drive around the mountains or wheat fields at night-time.
Australia's conservative Liberal Party had become notorious for resorting to xenophobic rants to garner additional support prior to an election.

Forms of the word: notoriety

Procrastinate

1. to put off till another day or time; defer; delay.

If we are going to reap benefits by promoting our tourism industry it would not be prudent to procrastinate.
One of the more bewildering peculiarities of tradesmen of any ilk is their tendency to procrastinate when it comes to doing their own thing around their own house.
If we procrastinate in settling on Mars, the aliens might get there before us.

Forms of the word: procrastinated, procrastinating, procrastination, procrastinator

Retaliate

1. to return like for like (especially for harm done); take reprisals.

It is totally commendable that our friends, the Kiwi's, have never sought to retaliate against Australia for bowling that "grubber".
Those Australian bull ants will actually bite you if you retaliate by stepping on their mates.
The collective free world retaliated against the so-called Islamic State, that was nothing but a non-religious political terror group.

Forms of the word: retaliated, retaliating, retaliation, retaliatory

Verify

1. to prove (something) to be true; confirm; substantiate.

The Indonesian police were able to verify that the vehicle belonged to the Bali bombers because of a unique identity number attached to the vehicle's differential.

2. to find out the truth or correctness of, especially by examination or comparison.

The Chinese sent their lunar explorer to the dark side of the moon to verify that there were no aliens there.
The autopsy would be conducted, despite the woman crashing into the tree, because the insurance companies will always want to verify the cause of death in trying to avoid a payout.

Forms of the word: verifiable, verifiably, verification, verified, verifying

Chapter 8

Abate

1. to make less; diminish.

International trade and commerce will eventually abate acts of terrorism as progress builds a better world for everyone.
We will not have any realistic prospect of preserving our precious forests until the demand for disposable chopsticks begins to abate.

2. to become less in strength etc.; decrease.

Before making the crossing, the travellers had to wait for the rain to abate and for the waters to recede.

Forms of the word: abatement

Adamant

1. firm in purpose or opinion; unyielding.

The girl used her manual wristwatch to determine the direction of north by pointing twelve at the sun and was adamant that the direction of north was midway to the hour hand.
Thomas Edison was adamant that the greatest invention of all time, that gave rise to so many forms of machinery, was the electric dynamo.
The Chinese government remained adamant that its foray into the South China Sea was not for military purposes.

Astounding

1. astound = to overcome with amazement.

There is nothing in New Zealand or Australia as astounding as the view of the Milford Valley when you exit the Homer Tunnel to drive toward Milford Sound.
Naturalists in England were astounded to find that the first specimen of an Australian platypus that they were able to study was, in fact, not a contrivance.
The clarity of the first photographs returned from the Mars rover “Spirit” was so clear, even the NASA scientists were astounded.

Atrocious

1. shockingly wicked or cruel; heinous; ruthless.

The President commented that the world had not seen such atrocious acts of violence since the Middle Ages.
The beheading of a young teenage boy for listening to popular music was one of the most atrocious acts ever perpetrated by terrorists.
The rape of women kidnapped by terrorists is one of the most heinous atrocities ever perpetrated upon one human being by another.

Forms of the word: atrociousness, atrocity

Candid

1. open and sincere.

He requested a reference from his former employer but she informed him in a very candid manner that, in his work, he did not handle volume very well – a veiled reference to his paltry work output.

2. fair; honest

It is important for marriage guidance counsellors to be prudent but also quite candid in everything they say.
The clairvoyant woman perceived considerable adversity in the young man's future, but she informed him tactfully and candidly, as it was his due karma.

Forms of the word: candidly

Complacent

1. **a feeling of quiet pleasure, especially with oneself.**

It would be perilous to become even just a little complacent about fire or snakes whilst wandering the Australian bush during summer.
The Chinese constructed their Great Wall of China because there was no complacency regarding the incursions by Mongols and barbarians.
If we continue to be complacent about the diminishing ice cap at the North Pole, we risk forcing our population of polar bears into extinction.

Forms of the word: complacency

Condone

1. **to pardon or overlook (an offence).**

The United Nations should never condone the actions of an aggressor against neighbouring countries.
If you want your children to be good people you should never condone any form of uncharitable behaviour between them.
Various governments around the world condone the continued exploration and development of gas reserves, supposedly as a transitional phase toward renewable energy, despite the substantial level of carbon pollution it causes.

Forms of the word: condoned, condoning

Contemplate

1. **to look at or view with marked attention; view thoughtfully.**

As we enter a new era of international trade, we will do well to contemplate how we intend to foster private enterprise and self-employment, when it is presently so perilous to take the necessary risks.
She did not have enough money to pay her tax account, but she took time to contemplate using what money she did have to purchase additional plant and equipment that could reduce her costs.

2. to have as a purpose; intend.

The President of the United States announced that in order to take the first steps into the universe, we should contemplate colonising Mars.

Forms of the word: contemplated, contemplating, contemplation, contemplative

Dearth

1. a very small supply; lack.

During France's Reign of Terror following the inception of the French Revolution, thousands of people were executed by guillotine, as there was no dearth of wealthy nobility.
There will never be a dearth of redback spiders under our Aussie dunny seats.
There seems to be an appalling dearth of wealthy people committed to philanthropy.

Delude

1. to mislead the mind or judgment of; deceive.

The Chinese government will probably continue to delude itself into believing that the United States will not assume a military motive in its incursion into the South China Sea.
If terrorists think they can impose their distorted version of sharia law upon rational western nations, they are deluding themselves.

If former President Donald Trump thinks the people will once again vote for such an obnoxious, bumptious, arrogant person he must be deluding himself.

Devious

1. not straightforward; tricky; deceptive; deceitful.

The aviation authorities contrived a devious plan to shift culpability for the tarmac collision away from the air traffic controllers and onto the flight crew.
His devious plan was to marry the Australian woman in Britain, then to divorce her in Australia after just a few years, simply so that he could gain entry to Australia.
Many insurance companies will contrive one devious strategy after another to fleece you of your money.

Dilemma

1. a situation in which a choice must be made between equally undesirable alternatives.

The dilemma we Earthlings face is whether to relocate to the coldness of Mars now, or to remain here on planet Earth until it runs out of resources.

2. any very difficult problem.

The dilemma confronting the people of the United States is whether they want President Donald Trump, or a normal person, as their next President.
The question of whether we should provide financial support to our inventors, or wait for another country to do so, seems to pose a considerable dilemma for us.

Expedite

1. to speed up the progress of; hasten.

You might create real wealth for yourself by expediting payments to your credit card - and investing what you save in interest payments.
Additional judges were appointed to the District Court in an attempt to expedite the process of litigation, which had become unduly delayed.
There is no doubt that we need to expedite the reverse engineering of spacecraft that come from other parts of the universe.

Forms of the word: expedited, expediting, expeditious

Feasible

1. able to be done or carried out.

The proposal to build a water pipeline through the middle of the Australian outback from Kununurra to Adelaide was entirely feasible.
The united effort of the nations involved in space exploration had determined that it was in fact feasible to place a person on Mars before the end of the century.
The feasibility study revealed that the proposed dam on the Congo River would provide electricity to the entire African continent.

Forms of the word: feasibility, feasibleness, feasibly

Lucid

1. shining or bright.

The planets Venus and Jupiter are clearly the most lucid of extra-terrestrial bodies in a clear night sky.

2. clear or transparent.

The teacher's explanation to the class, that they were about to study the theory of evolution because of the body of scientific knowledge that gave credibility to the theory, was a very lucid explanation.

3. easily understood.

The extremely low incidence of drug abuse among school children in private schools is a lucid example of how the threat of expulsion can nurture discipline.

4. with clear understanding; rational.

The mathematics teacher drew three circles on the board with the second overlapping the first and the third overlapping each of the first two as a very lucid presentation of a Venn diagram.

Precarious

1. dependent on conditions beyond one's control; uncertain; insecure.

The astronauts had landed safely on the moon and had completed their moonwalks knowing that the slightest fault with the re-launch would place them in a very precarious situation.

2. dangerous; perilous; risky.

The future of humanity will become extremely precarious should nuclear weapons fall into the hands of terrorists.
Borrowing more money to support an unviable business may place you in an even more precarious position.

Precipitant

1. falling or rushing headlong.

Though evidence of flowing water had been discovered on Mars it would be a little precipitant of NASA to send astronauts there straight away.

2. hasty; rash.

The program to release repeat offenders early under strictly supervised conditions was regarded by the group representing victims of crime as being somewhat precipitant.
The proposal to increase the goods and services tax was feared by the backbenchers as precipitant, given the likely electoral fallout.

Restrain

1. to hold back from action; keep in check or under control; keep down; repress.

It will be necessary to restrain on-field violence if we are going to encourage our youngsters into football.
The Australian people had decided to elect their President directly as a mechanism to restrain their politicians from feathering their own nests.
It goes without saying that we must restrain mining companies from exploring the Great Barrier Reef.

Forms of the word: restraining, restraint

Revert

1. to return, as to a former habit, belief, condition, subject, etc.

We have given free trade our best shot and it just won't work, so we may have to revert to exporting rather than importing.
Due to the increasing incidence of terrorism, some states within the USA decided to revert to execution by electric chair rather than by lethal injection.
Perhaps our entire system of government needs to revert to one of benevolent dictatorship.

Forms of the word: reversion, revertible

Tentative

1. of the nature of, or made or done as, a test or attempt to see what will happen; experimental.

The logging company had been given the all clear to remove forestry debris from the forest floor for wood chipping, but it was clearly only a tentative arrangement.
Permission had been granted for the company to continue fishing for southern blue-fin tuna, but it was a tentative measure to be reviewed at the end of the season.

2. unsure; cautious; diffident; hesitant.

She felt extremely tentative about allowing her ex-husband access to the children.

Forms of the word: tentatively

Chapter 9

Abrogate

1. to bring (a law, etc.) officially to an end; abolish; repeal

In its milestone 1992 Mabo decision, the High Court of Australia abrogated the validity of terra nullius – the concept that there were no rightful landowners in Australia prior to European settlement.
In view of the recently disclosed spate of child abuse cases perpetrated by Catholic clergy, teaching orders and many others too, the Catholic Pontiff decided he would strive to abrogate the requirement of Catholic priests to be single, celibate males.
In view of the numerous cases of gross incompetence and blatant negligence by so many Australian lawyers, the Australian government really had no choice but to abrogate advocates' immunity, with legislation.

Adhere

1. to be a follower or supporter.

Whilst at the bottom of the world, in New Zealand, it is best to shout a beer when it's your turn, because it is always wise to adhere to local norms.

2. to hold closely or firmly.

When you arrive at the "twelve second drop" atop McKinnon Pass on New Zealand's Milford Track, ensure that you adhere to the guide's instructions.
For reasons pertaining to the safety of ourselves and others we must all adhere to traffic rules.

Forms of the word: adherence, adherent

Adverse

1. threatening or hostile; antagonistic.

The Russian President persisted in delivering his most adverse comments, threatening the possibility of a nuclear response.

2. opposing one's interests or desire.

Life may seem to be a string of adverse occurrences for many people, but this may be due to their improvidence rather than to bad luck.

3. being or acting in an opposite direction.

Mariners preferred to sail their ships from west to east via the Cape of Good Hope because of the intensity of adverse winds if sailing from east to west.

Appease

1. to bring to a state of peace, quiet, or happiness.

A decision was made to upgrade the airport to international status in order to nurture tourism, to appease the displaced timber workers.
The introduction of enhanced childcare benefits by the government was an attempt to appease the women's electoral lobby prior to the election.

2. to satisfy.

Many nations introduced wage subsidies during the coronavirus lockdown to appease employers who wanted to retain their full-time workers.

Forms of the word: appeasement

Apprehensive

1. uneasy or fearful about something that may happen.

One might feel apprehensive before embarking on a four-day trek in New Zealand, about whether one has enough food to eat.
The backbenchers felt quite apprehensive about the Prime Minister calling a snap election.
All astronauts had felt apprehensive just prior to lift-off from the moon.

Avert

1. to prevent; ward off.

The airport was closed due to the fog to avert the possibility of a major catastrophe.
If we are friendly toward aliens, we could avert an inter-galactic conflict.
A more stringent enforcement of the Treaty of Versailles might have averted WWII.

Converge

1. to move towards each other.

There is a tendency for people of money power to converge upon one who is down, in the same way that vultures do.
Increasing productivity attributable to developments in information technology resulted from numerous corporations converging upon the Silicon Valley.
Metaphysical scientists have long recognised that God probably created the universe in such a way that the forces of nature could converge to give rise to evolutionary processes.

Forms of the word: converged, converging, convergent, convergence

Curtail

1. to cut short.

To promote tourism in this country we will need to curtail the tendency we have to charge exorbitant prices.
The whale cull continued unabated for decades before the dearth of whales forced the United Nations to enact a decree to curtail the slaughter.
The only thing that will curtail the expansion of terrorism is the education of the masses into the fundamentals of human rights.

Forms of the word: curtailment

Demise

1. death.

The demise of indigenous people the world over was attributable to imperialist ignorance of the need to recognise and respect other cultures.
It was the international community's abhorrence of the wholesale slaughter of blue whales that led to the demise of the whaling industry.
The demise of Tasmania's thylacine is another example of gross ignorance of governments and people alike.

Deterrent

1. something that has a discouraging effect.

The second atomic bomb was ostensibly dropped on the Japanese city of Nagasaki as a deterrent to the Soviet Union to transgress its boundaries.
There will always be a substantial degree of crime until the financial deterrent of monetary fines is replaced with constructive rehabilitation programs.
The proliferation of nuclear arms during the cold war was supposedly a deterrent to the adversary who amassed the same.

Forms of the word: deterrence

Enhance

1. **to raise to a higher degree; intensify; magnify.**

The academy of arts had sought assistance from established performers and artists with its schools' program as an attempt to enhance the image of the arts among young people.
The former Chilean President Salvador Allende introduced radical infrastructure programs to enhance the life prospects of his nation's poorest citizens.
The advent of the COVID-19 virus just might enhance cooperation between the world's leaders.

Forms of the word: enhanced, enhancing, enhancement

Extenuate

1. **to serve to make (a fault, offence, etc.) seem less serious.**

The judge handed down a lenient sentence to the first-time drug offender because the circumstances his peers had placed him into did extenuate his culpability.
Saddam claimed that extenuating circumstances pertaining to the possible rise of terrorism prompted him to implement his murderous regime.
The mercenary appealed (to be allowed to return home to the United States) on the extenuating circumstances surrounding his sortie into Somalia.

Forms of the word: extenuated, extenuating, extenuation

Gullible

1. **easily deceived or cheated.**

People who pay good money to attend seminars where somebody tells them how to get rich quickly may be somewhat gullible.

When it comes to having a swimming pool constructed in your back yard, make sure that you do not fall victim to a shyster who preys on gullible people.
Australia's kelpie will round up those poor hapless sheep that were just too gullible to realise that they were actually on their way to the market - as lamb chops.

Forms of the word: gullibility, gullibly

Instigate

1. to encourage (someone) to some (usually unacceptable) action.

The justice fighter was able to instigate the class action on behalf of the victims of business fraud, against the state government that had failed to enforce the law, by securing a pro bono financier.

2. to bring about by urging; foment.

You will need a lot of money to instigate legal proceedings as long as we do not have contingency arrangements with lawyers.
The people would be more inclined to instigate change towards a republic if the politicians would step aside and allow them to determine the questions they will vote on.

Forms of the word: instigation, instigator

Obscure

1. not clear or plain; uncertain.

Einstein's mathematical formula depicting the nexus between gravitational waves and the speed of light seemed a little obscure to most metaphysicians at the time.

It is possible to view just one other galaxy - the enormous Andromeda Galaxy – with the naked eye, but it is so far away that it appears to be just an obscure blur.

2. little seen or noticed.

The logging industry has a reputation for clear-felling copious amounts of pristine forest well away from the roads, to make its appalling effects somewhat obscure.

Forms of the word: obscured, obscurest, obscuring, obscurity

Preclude

1. to shut out; exclude; make impossible.

While we will not pro-actively promote the concept of New Zealand joining the Aussie Rules football league, we should not entirely preclude them from doing so.
Those Irish are trying to sway the game towards using a sissy round ball, but despite this we should not preclude them from international events.

2. to prevent (a person, etc.) from doing something.

We will have to preclude a team from Indonesia joining the Australian Football League because they don't have any tall ruckmen.

Forms of the word: precluded, precluding, preclusion

Pretentious

1. marked by supposed dignity or importance.

Of all the gala events in the world, there are none that so overtly portray the pretentious nature of people than do the academy awards.

2. making an exaggerated outward show; ostentatious.

Far too many young people now seek so much social media admiration from others that they have become quite pretentious.
All clairvoyant people are duly imbibed with a sense of meekness and humility, rather than pretentiousness.

Forms of the word: pretentiousness

Refute

1. to prove to be false, as an opinion, charge, etc.

I would refute the idea that a monster that had just been born would be sufficiently au fait with the laws to physics, to know that he was about to be sucked out of the spaceship window by a vacuum.

2. to prove (a person) to be in error.

The motorist was able to refute the infringement by producing video footage from a nearby business security system.
Sceptics will refute all creditable sightings of UFO's until one lands on their own front lawn.

Forms of the word: refutable, refutation, refuted, refuting

Resolve

1. to fix or settle on by choice and will; determine (to do something) (verb).

We must continue to explore deep space to resolve the question of whether or not life does exist throughout the universe.

2. to settle, determine, or state formally in a vote (verb).

The banks decided to resolve the litigation with a reasonable offer to all customers.

3. determination; firmness of purpose, especially to follow some course of action (noun).

The mountaineer had lost most of his toes to frostbite, but through his enormous resolve he continued to climb the world's highest peaks.

Forms of the word: resolved, resolving, resolvable

Vulnerable

1. able to be hurt or wounded.

The taxi drivers met with the Minister of Transport to lobby for additional security features, as they were far too vulnerable without safety screens.
As long as we are confined to just one planet, we will be vulnerable to self-extermination.

2. not protected against emotional hurt; highly sensitive.

This big tree made it to the top against a lot of other would-be trees that became rather stunted, because they were too vulnerable in a merciless forest of survival.

Forms of the word: vulnerability

Chapter 10

Abet

1. to help or encourage (usually something undesirable).

The high priests sought the assistance of Judas to abet their capture of Jesus.
The French Monarchy abetted the cause of the new world colonies against British rule, with financial assistance.
Invariably ruthless dictators are abetted by their military establishment, as the top-ranking officers are financially rewarded.

Ascertain

1. to find out by examination, or testing, so as to know as certain; determine.

If you are going to establish a new business, it is wise to develop a business plan to ascertain your likely revenue and expenditure.
In order to construct a bridge across the ravine, it was necessary to ascertain whether the trees on each side would hold the weight.
Before we do travel to planets around other stars, we will need to ascertain whether the locals are friendly.

Forms of the word: ascertainable, ascertainment

Assert

1. to state as true; affirm; declare.

The President of the United States appeared in an international telecast to assert that the blitz against transnational corporate taxation evaders would be enhanced with considerable resolve.

2. to defend (claims, rights, etc.).

The recalcitrant nation had not adhered to the United Nations charter and had subsequently forced the allies to assert their authority.

3. to put (oneself) forward boldly.

Building construction sites are no place for shrinking violets - you may have to assert yourself and stick up for your rights.

Forms of the word: asserted, asserting, assertion, assertive

Concede

1. to admit as true, fair or proper.

The Minister for Conservation was forced to concede that much of the supposed preserved area of forest was actually denuded farms, gravel pits and even rubbish tips.

2. to admit defeat.

Neanderthal people who lived in Europe more than twenty thousand years ago were forced to concede to the more intelligent Homo sapiens people.

3. to give in, yield.

The melting glaciers in the Himalayas are giving rise to glacial lakes which eventually burst their banks and flood local villages, forcing local people to concede that would need to move.

Forms of the word: conceded, conceding, concession

Culminate

1. to reach the highest point.

Our government's priority to nurture innovation should culminate in more export income, more businesses and more jobs.

It may be a long season but there is no doubt that when it culminates with the Australian Football League grand final in September, it has all been worthwhile.
Hopefully the advertising campaign by entrepreneurs in the hospitality industry culminates in luring tourists back to Christchurch.

Forms of the word: culminated, culminating, culmination

Divert

1. to turn aside or from a path or course; deflect.

The Hoover dam was constructed to divert the waters of the mighty Colorado River toward farming lands.

2. to set (traffic) on a detour.

There has recently been considerable need to divert traffic since the advent of major road infrastructure investment to make our road systems more efficient.

3. to draw off to a different object, purpose, etc.

The teachers introduced 'values education' that focused on family relationships in an attempt to divert the attention of the students away from peer pressure that had led them into drug abuse.

Entail

1. to bring on by necessity or as a result.

You may need to seek advice on just what your workplace agreement will entail in terms of long service leave and maternity leave.
The restoration of confidence in the small business sector entails providing people who dare to take a risk with adequate levels of security.
You might need to ask your lawyer specifically what services his horrendous quote actually entails.

Exemplify

1. to serve as an example of.

She had fallen ill but the CEO provided her with additional paid leave because he was confident that she would exemplify everything an employer could wish for in an employee.
The helicopter had gone into a spin over the Grand Canyon, but the pilot was of such exemplary skill that he manoeuvred his way safely to the ground.
The top student athlete devoted so much time to studying that he exemplified an ideal balance between sporting and academic pursuits.

Forms of the word: exemplification, exemplificative

Inkling

1. a slight suggestion; hint.

She developed an inkling that her boyfriend was two-timing from the way that he would no longer look into her eyes.
New Zealand's TranzAlpine train ride from Christchurch to Greymouth provides just an inkling of the enthralling sights this amazing country has to offer.

2. an uncertain idea; notion.

While she did not know for certain if her husband was organizing a surprise party for her, she had an inkling that he was from the number of phone calls he was receiving from other women.

Inordinate

1. not within proper limits; excessive.

The number of individual plants on the planet Earth is surely an inordinate amount.

One of the main problems of modern-day economies is that if governments are not sufficiently frugal, there will be an inordinate number of servants on the public payroll performing dubious functions.
Thanks to the Hubble Deep Space Field, we now know there is an inordinate number of galaxies in the universe.

Intransigent

1. keeping firmly to one's own ideas or position; uncompromising; irreconcilable.

You bought your tickets but when you arrived there were some really intransigent people occupying your seats.
Neither side was going to give ground in this battle of the waterfront with both the unions and the intransigent company being called before the Arbitration Commission for a decision.
Like many intransigent dictators before him, Libya's Muammar Gaddafi was deposed by his own people.

Forms of the word: intransigence

Meticulous

1. careful about small details.

The Benedictine Monk had written a large number of books with the most meticulous calligraphy.
Now that they can squeeze approximately thirteen thousand transistors across the width of a human hair, IBM needs to be very meticulous about dust particles in its production line.
The former Queen of England was always meticulous regarding her presentation – wearing a new gown every day.

Forms of the word: meticulously

Perturbed

1. to disturb or disquiet greatly in mind; agitate.

The woman had trekked several hours to the overnight hut on the Rees-Dart track and was very perturbed to find that the hut was overcrowded.
One has very good reason to feel perturbed when one learns that the little pin prick on the buttock whilst utilizing the ablution block at the local country football ground, was that infamous little redback spider.
The President was quite perturbed to learn that the Russians were providing the errant Syrian government with weapons.

Forms of the word: perturbable

Predicament

1. an unpleasant, trying, or dangerous situation.

The trekkers set off in perfect weather conditions, but a sudden blizzard had left them in such a predicament, they decided to turn back.
Sailing out to sea without adequate life gear can leave one in a terrible predicament, should the weather turn sour.
The Apollo 13 astronauts found themselves in a life-threatening predicament following the explosion.

Preposterous

1. directly opposite to nature, reason, or common sense; absurd.

To continue to populate the world without providing third world countries with adequate birth control is entirely preposterous.
To land a crewed craft on Mars and expecting to have a contingency plan should a return lift off fail is a preposterous idea.
Allowing drug users to grow their own cannabis, supposedly for personal use only, is a totally preposterous proposition.

Quell

1. to put an end to (disorder, mutiny etc.); suppress; extinguish.

A more equitable distribution of the world's wealth would go a long way in our quest to quell the radicalisation of young people in poverty-stricken countries.

2. to conquer; subdue.

One nation had shot down an aircraft belonging to its neighbouring nation, but the United Nations Peacekeeping Force stepped in to quell any possible escalation into all out warfare.

3. to quiet or calm (feeling, etc.).

The league anticipated trouble at the soccer match between the two ethnic groups, but it held a typical Aussie barbeque beforehand, in an attempt to quell any unruly or rollicking behaviour.

Refrain

1. to keep oneself back.

Could all smokers please destroy their own lungs but refrain from contributing to the declining health of others.
Whilst out on a fishing boat in shark infested waters it may be wise to refrain from throwing out berley from the rear gangplank.
People who live in glass houses should refrain from throwing stones.

Resolute

1. firmly fixed or determined; set in purpose or opinion.

Not to be deterred, the United States President made certain that his country would stand resolute in the fight against terrorism.

The footballers were under siege late into the last quarter and were in real danger of losing the match, but the backline stood resolute in the crisis.
Though General George Custer's men were resolute to the end, they were simply outnumbered.

Forms of the word: resolutely

Salutary

1. doing good; wholesome; beneficial.

As consumers become increasingly health conscious the loss of customers will surely become a salutary lesson for people in the food industry who do not wear gloves.
The low score with which she was credited in her university exam was a salutary lesson for her to read her textbooks rather than to party too hard.
His defeat at the election was a salutary reminder that in politics the electorate regards a change as conducive to good government.

Suppress

1. to put an end to the activities of (a person, group of people, etc.).

The Rolling Stones were forced to sing amended lyrics on the Ed Sullivan show as the middle-class establishment tried to suppress youth sexual expression.

2. to keep in or repress (a feeling, smile, groan, etc.).

When travelling on public transport, it is always a good idea to suppress the release of flatulence.

3. to put an end to (a revolt, etc.) by force; quell; subdue.

The North Korean dictator was merely a puppet to his military regime that constantly suppressed any attempts by the Red Cross to ascertain the extent of starvation.

Forms of the word: suppression, suppressor, suppressive

Chapter 11

Abhorrent

1. causing hate and disgust; detestable.

The use of chemical weapons by Saddam Hussein against his own people was a most abhorrent atrocity.
It is with peculiar flippancy that we allow any children anywhere in this world to witness the abhorrence of war.
The slaughter of innocent people in Bosnia and Rwanda are two most recent examples of the abhorrence of genocide.

Forms of the word: abhor, abhorred, abhorring, abhorrence

Acumen

1. quickness of understanding; keen judgment.

The Aboriginal liaison officer displayed considerable acumen in acquiring artefacts from his clients to export for sale in New Zealand.
It was only through her ingenuity and acumen that she had established a thriving business making muffins for distribution through supermarkets.
His business acumen was clearly evident from his development of the computer spreadsheet.

Coerce

1. to force or compel to do something.

You cannot demand somebody to sign an insurance policy document, but by disturbing them with appropriate questions you can coerce them into doing so.
The indigenous American communities were removed from their homelands by the United States Army and coerced into relocating to barren desert lands.

The lawyer quoted horrific figures for his future services to handle the case, in order to coerce his client into accepting the offer of settlement.

Forms of the word: coerced, coercing, coercion, coercive

Conceited

1. having too high an opinion of one's abilities, importance, etc.

Yes, she had won the beauty contest but her avoidance of her best friends in favour of others associated with the magazine was a totally conceited response.
The new President certainly had a rather conceited opinion of his own understanding of the protocols of international diplomacy.
Psychic ability is normally bestowed on very meek people rather than people who are conceited.

Forms of the word: conceitedness

Contingent

1. dependent for existence, occurrence, character, etc., on something not yet certain; conditional.

Many ex-offenders will not disclose their crime to a prospective employer because obtaining a job may be contingent upon not having a criminal record.
Colonising the universe will be contingent upon developing a propulsion system that can warp spacetime around our future spacecraft.

2. happening by chance or without known cause; fortuitous; accidental.

Though she was a person of exemplary business acumen who had once been bankrupted, in a contingent outcome she won the lottery.

Forms of the word: contingency

Conversant

1. familiar by use or study.

The businesswoman was sufficiently conversant with leasing to enquire about the minimum duration for the lease of the video monitoring equipment.
Astronauts returning a space shuttle to Earth need to be more than a little conversant with the angle of the dangle.
After becoming the United States President, Donald Trump showed he was not exactly conversant with normal protocols of most things.

Detract

1. to take away part, as from quality, value, or regard.

Though he served a prison sentence for defrauding his company, let us not detract from the contribution this man made in winning the America's Cup for Australia.
Acceding to popular demand would only result in God's church on earth standing accused of detracting from the indelibility of ultimate truth.
Our former Prime Minister addressed the ultra-conservative audience by stating that same sex marriage would detract from marriage as an institution within society.

Forms of the word: detractor, detraction

Diverse

1. different; unlike.

Our diverse range of Australian built motor cars includes basic and luxurious sedans, station wagons (for people with kids), the great Aussie ute (surfboard, tools, dog) and the legendary panel van (surfboard, tools, girlfriend).

2. of various kinds or forms; multiform.

We should not rely so much on our mineral deposits for our wealth but nurture a diverse manufacturing economy too.
The corporation bought farms and manufacturing businesses, in order to diversify its portfolio.

Divulge

1. to disclose or reveal (something private, secret, or unknown).

The insurance company decided to pay one troublemaker who was making threats of legal action, but did not divulge this to other policy holders.
You do not have to divulge your identity to a police officer unless the officer first provides you with a reason for wanting to know who you are.
Catholic priests are under strict instructions to never divulge the sins of a confessor.

Forms of the word: divulged, divulging, divulgence

Eradicate

1. to remove or destroy totally; extirpate.

The introduction of the cane toad to Queensland to eradicate the fire moth was an abysmal failure.
Though myxomatosis had been largely rendered harmless to rabbits, that had developed immunity to the disease, the new Calicivirus was developed to eradicate this rabbit vermin.
Thankfully, football codes have gone a long way to eradicating head high contact.

Forms of the word: eradicated, eradicating, eradication

Expedient

1. fit or suitable for a particular purpose or situation.

The Australian Liberal Party leader campaigned against the amendment to the Constitution to recognize Aboriginal people but his expedient motive was to garner more support at the next federal election from conservative citizens.

2. based on consideration of advantage or interest, rather than right.

It was for reasons of commercial expediency that the superannuation fund manager sent the insurance policy details to the worker's former address.
The police officer was trying to rush the woman in writing her report because he had other things to do, but she detected his expedient approach.

Forms of the word: expediency, expediently

Fallacy

1. a deceptive, misleading, or false idea, belief, etc.

Many of the people trapped into losing their assets in the retail sector fall victim to the fallacy that shops must be doing well if they are operating.
The use of glossolalia as the supposed gift of tongues by Pentecostal Christians, is regarded by linguistic science as a total fallacy.

2. a misleading or unsound argument.

The notion that only the good die young is an absolute fallacy, but one meant to comfort the bereaved.

Forms of the word: fallibility, fallible

Impasse

1. a position from which there is no escape.

A collective of exporters of lamb lobbied their own government to impose duties on the countries that had levied tariffs on lamb imports, but they met an impasse with their own government's reluctance to retaliate.
All attempts to cross Australia's Blue Mountains had come to an impasse until Wentworth, Blaxland and Lawson succeeded in 1813.
The attempt by the company to break the union representation on the docks struck an impasse when overseas trained workers were prevented from entering the country.

Imperative

1. not to be avoided; necessary (adj.).

In order to foster a community of cooperative young people, it is imperative to involve them in decision making from an early age.
Some will scoff at the enormous cost of space exploration, but it really is imperative to find answers to the evolution of the universe if we can.

2. anything which must be done, obtained, etc. (noun).

We must do everything possible to arrest the problem of the melting Arctic ice in order to save our population of polar bears, as an imperative.

Inculcate

1. to place in the mind by repeated statement; instil.

The government had somewhat belatedly funded a media campaign on the devastating effects of the proliferation of chronic gambling, in an attempt to inculcate an aversion to gambling among young people.
It was true that Australians had become the world's highest users of mobile phones because the telephone companies were able to inculcate the perception of using mobiles to overcome the tyranny of distance.
We must focus on how best to inculcate an understanding of how detestable domestic violence really is.

Forms of the word: inculcated, inculcating

Innocuous

1. not harmful; harmless.

The tall bulky ruckman was a frightening sight to the opposition players but being a Christian man, he was innocuous enough when it came to on field skirmishes.
Several of Australia's lizards will rise up and flare their neck in a quite frightening pose if they are threatened but they are totally innocuous, without any venom or even sharp teeth.
By virtue of the frequency of their visitations to earth over centuries, aliens have displayed how innocuous they really are.

Malice

1. the desire to hurt or harm another person.

One of life's true indicators of character is the extent to which we feel malice towards other people.
The religious wars that became known as "The Crusades" that took place between the 11th and 15th centuries in Europe and Jerusalem, involved the malicious, indiscriminate murder of innocent people for their religious beliefs.
The people of Iraq certainly felt malice toward Saddam Hussein for all the oppressive years they had endured under his dictatorship.

Forms of the word: malicious, maliciously

Reiterate

1. to repeat; say or do again or repeatedly.

He had said it all before, but the judge had to reiterate to the convicted that his lengthy sentence was to deter others from violence against the elderly.
The President stood before the press gallery to reiterate his earlier comments that his country would not accede to the demands of terrorists.
The alien leaders once again addressed the Russian President to reiterate the need to disarm his country's stockpile of nuclear weapons.

Forms of the word: reiterated, reiterating, reiteration

Tangible

1. able to be touched or felt by touch; material; substantial.

There was nothing obscure about the plan to plant one billion trees in the salt affected farming area as the results would be tangible enough in due course.

2. real or actual, rather than imaginary.

The televangelist was notorious for conjuring supposed miracles by coercing stooges to role play for money, but there were no tangible cases that were medically verifiable.

3. definite; not vague.

Who can blame people for being sceptical about religious veneration when, in a world troubled by so much conflict, there seems to be a dearth of tangible answers to prayers.

Forms of the word: tangibility

Vehement

1. angry or bitter.

The United States President delivered a vehement criticism of his Russian counterpart for instigating the Crimean conflict.

2. passionate; strongly emotional.

The Catholic Pontiff was vehement in his criticism of people who rationalised their violence with exhortations to religion.

3. (of actions) marked by great energy; forceful.

With our computer virus and a nuclear bomb, we delivered a vehement response to those aliens who tried to invade us.

Forms of the word: vehemence, vehemently

Chapter 12

Aberration

1. a change or departure from what is right, normal, or true.

The tilt of our planet Earth to more than twenty degrees, caused by a cataclysmic collision with another planet and which gives rise to our seasons, seems to be an aberration within the universe.
The Senator explained away his philandering with his very attractive secretary as a mere aberration of his true character.
As the universe is still expanding, the impending collision of the giant Milky Way and Andromeda galaxies might be considered as a mere aberration of the cosmos.

Allay

1. put at rest; quiet.

The statements by the Treasurer to allay people's fears of termination of funding were correctly seen by some as a kite flying exercise.
The boy was accompanied to the outside lavatory by his grandmother to allay his fears that the spider webs, therein, were not those of the notorious redback spider.
The United States government's constant denials about Roswell have done nothing to allay our concerns that aliens have indeed visited the earth.

Amorphous

1. without fixed shape or form.

The process of evolution is based upon survival of the fittest because of the amorphous nature of the gene pool of every species.
It was because of the ambivalence of conservative governments that funding to remote Aboriginal communities was always in an amorphous state.

Our weather changes from day to day because of the constantly amorphous conditions in the atmosphere and in our oceans.

Coherent

1. having natural or well-reasoned connection of parts; consistent.

The student became totally adept at essay writing because she approached the task in a structured and coherent manner.
Though she had been struck by a car that failed to stop, she was sufficiently coherent to be able to give the police a description.
The member of Parliament made a rather babbling, incoherent response to questions about his relationship with his secretary.

Forms of the word: coherence

Deviate

1. to turn aside (from a way or course); swerve; digress.

The Apollo 11 astronauts had to deviate from their intended flightpath to the moon, in order to avoid a strange looking spaceship.
When early humans started to cook meat, wolves decided to deviate away from hunting to follow them and, due to the amorphous nature of the gene pool, eventually gave rise to the modern-day dog.
Inveterate perpetrators of crime are considered by society to be deviants.

Forms of the word: deviant, deviation

Elaborate

1. worked in great detail; complicated (adj.).

The project to construct the Three Gorges Dam on the Yangtze River in China was an extremely elaborate engineering feat.

NASA's James Webb Telescope, launched in December of 2021, is surely one of the most elaborate scientific instruments ever created.

2. to give (added) detail (verb).

Since the Congressman's testimony under oath really didn't make sense, he was asked to elaborate on exactly what he meant by "sexual relations".

Embroil

1. to involve, as in a fight, strife, etc.

The mining company's failure to concede that the indigenous people's rights entitled them to substantial compensation, only served to embroil the company in a protracted legal delay.
It makes sense to leave your work problems at work rather than bringing them home to embroil your partner.

2. to throw into confusion; complicate.

The construction of artificial islands in the South China Sea will eventually embroil all of China's trading relationships.

Forms of the word: embroilment

Entice

1. to attract by exciting hope or desire.

As soon as you walk into some jeans shops, you know they are going to entice you into buying with a bit of hard sell about how good you look.
The retail property developer would entice young couples to lease premises in his new shopping centre with blatant lies about estimated customer numbers.
Our western lifestyle will gradually entice young people in radicalised middle eastern countries to pursue truly democratic government.

Forms of the word: enticed, enticement, enticing

Envisage

1. to form a mental image of, especially a future event.

In order to protect humanity, the world's leaders need to envisage what a renegade terrorist group might be planning.
The Palestinian people have fought so desperately for a homeland because they envisage living together in peace.
With so many billions of planets in the known universe, it is difficult for us to envisage what conditions will be like on the surface of most.

Facade

1. an appearance, especially a misleading one.

The sardonic smile of the Presidential candidate was clearly false and indicative that his visit to the remote Apache community was a simply a facade.
The mining company's stated priority for health and safety was exposed as a facade of smoke and mirrors when it retrenched all safety personnel before any others.
Arabian sheiks typically convey a facade of moral restraint within their own countries but flout such beliefs while visiting Western nations, flagrantly indulging in the consumption of alcohol and women.

Fortuitous

1. happening by chance or by good luck; accidental.

Russia is the largest country in the world by area, followed by Canada, China, the United States, Brazil and Australia - but fortuitously we don't live there.

They lost their wallet on the side of the road somewhere between Wyalkatchem and Mukinbudin and it was remarkably fortuitous that a marathon runner in training had noticed it.
Fortuitously, we eventually realised that the alien visitors had actually come here to protect us from destroying our planet Earth.

Forms of the word: fortuitously, fortuity

Fraught

1. involving; attended (with); full (of).

White water rafting in Yosemite National Park without adequate buoyancy equipment is an activity fraught with danger.
Venturing into the Amazon jungle without an experienced guide would be fraught with peril.
Her heart was fraught with grief as her very first boyfriend had left her for another girl.

Impede

1. to slow down in movement or progress by means of obstacles; obstruct; hinder.

The Great Walls of China are actually a series of walls constructed over a period spanning centuries, to impede the progress of aggressors.
There is no doubt that government taxes levied on share market transactions constitute a significant impediment to international companies investing in our country.
The mining company introduced autonomous, driverless dump trucks but it would be folly to impede any form of progress.

Forms of the word: impeded, impeding, impediment

Inevitable

1. not able to be avoided or escaped; certain or necessary.

We may not like to think so, but it is inevitable that nature will devise its own form of vengeance upon a species that dominates the planet so.
That so many of us New Zealanders will move to Australia for opportunities relating to employment, housing, entertainment, women and beer is an inevitable aspect of trans-Tasman life.
It seems inevitable that the Zika virus will affect people on every continent.

Forms of the word: inevitability, inevitableness, inevitably

Placate

1. to make calm, peaceful; appease.

The Australian government finally apologised to its Aboriginal people in order to placate their feelings of animosity over being dispossessed of their land.
Terrorists are not receptive to being placated.
It seems little can be done to placate the angst between the Israeli people and Palestinians.

Forms of the word: placated, placating, placatory

Rescind

1. to withdraw formally; annul; revoke; repeal; abrogate.

In the light of the enormous backlash from the Confederation of Industry, the government decided to rescind the unfair dismissal legislation.
The golf club was forced to rescind sections of its constitution and so allow women to play on Saturdays.
In light of the new evidence the High Court invoked a rescission of the deed of settlement to allow the victims of the scam to sue the banks again.

Forms of the word: rescindable, rescission

Semantic

1. relating to signs or meaning.

The police report that the fraudsters had paid tax on their profit was blatantly semantic, as it was a significantly lower profit than the profit they claimed to the purchaser of the business.
The Senator was resorting to semantics to explain why he had failed to disclose his conflict of interest in relation to the mining venture.
The Product Disclosure Statement now circulated by all retail superannuation funds in Australia was laden with nightmare clauses dressed up with semantics contrived by devious lawyers and psychologists.

Solace

1. (something that gives) comfort in sorrow or trouble (noun).

When it is all over, there will be but one solace for humankind - there may be some of us left on a spaceship somewhere.
The priest was able to provide solace to the grieving family with his words from the holy Gospel.

2. to comfort, console or cheer (verb).

She was suffering so much stress in her life that she regularly went "bush" on Sundays, as the gentle breeze in the trees solaced her.

Subservient

1. (of persons, their conduct, etc.) very submissive; servile; obsequious.

Father Knows Best is unlikely to make a return to the television screen, because Jim's wife, Margaret, was so totally subservient to him.
One of the bases upon which so many young people are brought up within conservative religious education systems, is to be overly subservient to authority.
The impact of today's technology will gradually erode the level of subservience of women in many middle eastern nations.

Forms of the word: subservience

Transpire

1. to happen, or take place.

The introduction of "values education" in our high schools should transpire into stronger social bonds within the wider community.
She established her advisory service to warn people of the perils of shopping centre tenancy and to see what transpired from this, her first foray into a consultancy business.
We really should bite the bullet, put some money up to sponsor some good innovations onto the market and, if good fortune transpires, we then utilise some of the profits to sponsor the next round.

Forms of the word: transpired, transpiring, transpiration

Chapter 13

Accede

1. to agree; consent; yield.

The shopping centre developer had no choice but to accede to his tenants' demands because he had circulated dubious information.
The granting of rights to the alternative telephone provider to utilise the local Telstra network was an accession that would have immense benefit for the entire country.
The Parliament was ready to accede and include reference to prior ownership of the land by the indigenous Australians, within the new constitution.

Aloof

1. at a distance, but within view; withdrawn (adv.)

Her best friend suggested that, as the young man had already made a play for herself, her friend remain somewhat aloof from him.

2. disinterested; unsympathetic; reserved (adj.)

One characteristic of unemployed people who are not genuinely seeking employment is that they will remain as aloof as possible from their case managers.
The Archbishop could see no problem at all with those Welsh hymns composed in the 19th century for his congregation, because he was totally aloof from the needs of modern-day young people.

Forms of the word: aloofness

Coalesce

1. to unite so as to form one mass, community, etc.

Despite the demise of eastern-bloc European socialism, some redneck minded activists persist in coalescing within the union movement.
You can always expect people who want to drink Guinness to coalesce around a good Irish tavern.
It may seem a little strange how planets tend to coalesce around a star rather than being autonomous, but that is how our universe evolves.

Forms of the word: coalesced, coalescing, coalescence, coalescent

Contravene

1. to come or be in conflict with; go or act counter to; oppose.

Governments had established legislation to control taxation avoidance, but transnational corporations persisted to contravene the law, because the legislation was not vigilantly enforced between nations.
The transfer of billions of dollars to offshore tax havens was an unashamed contravention of the spirit of taxation legislation.

2. to violate, infringe or transgress.

If you wish to keep your driver's licence, it is good policy to contravene road rules as few times as possible.

Forms of the word: contravened, contravening, contravention

Contrive

1. to plan with cleverness; devise; invent.

The proposal by the Fijian government to introduce daylight saving for the purpose of circumventing New Zealand's claim to be the first country to enter the new millennium, was a blatant attempt to contrive a claim to fame.

2. to form schemes or designs; plan; plot.

Critics claimed the invasion of Iraq over weapons of mass destruction was an attempt to contrive a justification, when the true motive was about access to oil supplies.
The interpretation of taxation legislation by the transnational corporation's lawyers was adjudged by the High Court as a total contrivance.

Forms of the word: contrivable, contrived, contriving

Cursory

1. short and rapid, without noticing details; superficial.

They didn't want to encourage the bikies to stop at their roadhouse whilst on their country jaunts, so they provided the bikies with only a cursory service.
He didn't succeed at door to door selling of telephone systems because he really wasn't sufficiently assertive and made merely a cursory attempt to procure a sale.
The defence counsel was castigated by the presiding judge for giving what the judge considered just cursory lip service in defending his client.

Forms of the word: cursorily

Detest

1. to feel distaste for; hate.

The entire world had come to detest the heinous atrocities perpetrated against innocent people by terrorists.
The actions of the bikies in detaining the woman within their enclave against her will were entirely detestable.
What more detestable act of crime could there possibly be than the molestation and murder of children?

Forms of the word: detestable

Explicit

1. clearly and fully expressed.

President Dwight Eisenhower issued an explicit instruction for the "son of a bitch in charge of Area 51" to hand over the files, or he would come in there himself with the First National Army from Colorado.
Unbeknown to the President of the United States of America, the aliens had already issued their own explicit instructions that their presence here on planet Earth was not to be disclosed, for fear of undermining religious beliefs.

2. definite in expression; outspoken.

The incoming President of FIFA was quite explicit in his pledge to stamp out corruption.

Frivolous

1. of little or no weight, worth, or importance.

Trying to convince American people who follow baseball that cricket is a far superior game, may be an absolutely frivolous exercise.

2. lacking seriousness or sense.

The cane toad had become so pervasive in Queensland that the Minister for Agriculture's suggestion to collect them for bounty was a totally frivolous idea.
It would be totally frivolous to expect many American people to consider the concept of Old Earth creationism, rather than Young Earth creationism.

Forms of the word: frivolity

Fruition

1. the reaching of a goal or production of results.

You can self-actualise by bringing your lifelong dreams to fruition with strategic contemplation, planning, action and reflection.
By exploiting thousands of labourers, the Pharaoh finally brought the construction of his pyramid to fruition.
Clearly the way ahead for our economy is to expedite the development of all forms of innovation to fruition.

Implicate

1. to involve as being concerned in a matter, affair, condition, etc.

The police had such compelling evidence against the drug runner that he sought to implicate others to attenuate his own culpability.
If working for the taxation office, it may be advisable not to divulge information to the press that might implicate you in a breach of confidentiality.
The Royal Commission into child abuse tried to implicate the Archbishop who had shunted the offending priests around to different parishes.

Forms of the word: implicated, implicating

Inherent

1. existing in something as a permanent and inseparable part or quality.

An inherent aspect of our nature as human beings is our ability to perceive the existence of an intelligent deity who has contrived the mathematical powers of the universe.
There is an inherent part of human nature that compels us to contemplate the origin of the universe and what the universe is expanding into.
We need to ask ourselves whether goodness or evil is the dominant inherent force within our hearts.

Ominous

1. telling of approaching evil; threatening.

The hole in the ozone layer over Australia was a far more ominous warning for humankind than the scientists had disclosed.
It was probably inevitable, but the development of nuclear arms by many of the world's lesser powers poses an ominous warning for humankind.
The extinction of so many thousands of species of fauna in recent times is an ominous sign that more will follow due to our negligence.

Forms of the word: ominously

Pedantic

1. to put too much importance on small details.

The umpire had been quite pedantic to award a penalty simply because the fullback had sworn at him.
Whilst in New Zealand's Milford Sound, it may be just a trifle pedantic to argue which of the eminent and majestic Mt. Christina's three daughters is the highest.
The chief executive officer was being quite pedantic by informing his secretary that she had actually worked about fifteen minutes less than she had claimed.

Procure

1. to get, especially by care, effort, or the use of special means.

The young lad would visit the house across the road from where he lived and try to procure a small kiss from the teenage girl who lived there.
NASA sent the Lunar Reconnaissance Orbiter to the moon to map the moon's surface and to procure photographs of remnants of the first lunar landing in July 1969.

When the aliens finally revealed themselves, NASA did everything it could to procure their anti-gravity technology.

Forms of the word: procured, procuring, procurable, procurement

Provoke

1. to anger or annoy.

We must not provoke aliens into a conflict because their technology is far superior to ours.

2. to stir up or arouse (action or feeling).

President Eisenhower arrived at Area 51 with the First National Army to provoke a confrontation with his presiding General, but he found that the alien leaders, themselves, were in charge.

3. to excite (a person etc.) to action.

The renegade dictator endeavoured to provoke his population into believing that they were engaged in a religious war with the West.

Retrograde

1. returning to an earlier and lesser state.

To renew the practice of removing children from their parents because the parents suffer from mental disability would constitute a gravely retrograde step.
The space shuttle commander considered casting the astronaut from the spacecraft to find his own way home, but Houston advised this would be a retrograde step in her career.
Allowing Russia to dominate any former Soviet Union nations would be retrograde in the extreme.

Sanctimonious

1. making a show of holiness; affecting sanctity.

The old priest was sufficiently experienced in human relations to know that Christians who are overtly sanctimonious are at risk of sexual temptation.
The Presidential candidate obtrusively put himself forward as quite a sanctimonious character – until his former concubines spoke up against him.
Jesus was scathingly critical of those sanctimonious high priests who made a display of their piety while being devoid of love for people.

Forms of the word: sanctimony

Ulterior

1. being beyond what is seen or declared openly; intentionally kept concealed.

Did the President of the oil-consuming country have an ulterior motive for providing military assistance to the oil exporting country?
There was clearly an ulterior purpose behind the Parliament's decision to allow continued tax minimization through negative gearing of domestic rental property, as most of our politicians are driving their truck through the same.
The chief executive officer gave his attractive secretary a glowing reference, but he clearly had an ulterior motive.

Vindictive

1. having or showing a revengeful spirit.

Despite their stronger social bonding to each other, Australia's farmers can be very vindictive toward their own politicians who are seen to abandon them.
The actions of the ethnic group in seeking vengeance for the atrocities perpetrated against their own were understandable but were clearly vindictive.
It is gravely unwise to be vindictive toward members of your own immediate family.

Chapter 14

Admonish

1. to tell of, or reprove for, a fault, duty etc.

The employer was normally an amicable person, but in this instance, where one of his staff used the company vehicle whilst intoxicated, he had no choice but to admonish her severely.
That woman space shuttle commander sought to admonish her fellow astronaut by confiscating his calendar of bikini girls.
Corporate managers who admonish rather than castigate their employees generally engender greater team morale.

Forms of the word: admonition

Anomalous

1. varying from the usual type or form; abnormal; irregular.

On the face of it, the inconsistent application of law between men - who are given longer jail sentences - and women, seems entirely anomalous.
It appears totally anomalous that, despite the best efforts of governments through affirmative action legislation, women continue to be under-represented in corporate board rooms.
The facility to reduce one's tax by negative gearing of domestic rental income is an anomaly that favours wealthy people, including our politicians, who avail of this devious mechanism themselves.

Forms of the word: anomaly

Compromise

1. the settlement of differences by giving way on both sides (noun).

On the question of compensation to Aboriginal people with genuine Native Title claims, both the mining companies and the Aboriginal communities should arrive at a compromise.
The loggers eventually agreed to a compromise on the forestry strategy by starting to plant trees that they really could call their own when it came time to fell them, rather than chopping down trees that belong to all of us.

2. to lay open to danger, dishonour, suspicion, scandal, etc. (verb).

Successive United States governments have not been willing to compromise their standing in the eyes of the community by revealing that the Roswell incident did involve an alien spacecraft.

Forms of the word: compromised, compromising

Credulous

1. ready to believe things, especially without good reasons.

You really do have to be just a little credulous to buy something on hire purchase without knowing all relevant details of the finance plan.
Weirdos continue to post supposed photographs of life forms on Mars on the internet, but they usually make money from credulous people, with internet advertising in the process.
Since the vast majority of the human race grow up, live and die subscribing to the same belief systems as their family, perhaps credulity is the fundamental basis of socialisation.

Forms of the word: credulity, credulousness

Decimate

1. to destroy a great number or amount of.

The decision by hordes of money moguls in Hong Kong, the United States and Japan to withdraw capital from south-east Asia during the global financial crisis, had decimated those economies.
The earthquake and subsequent tsunami had completely decimated the coastal villages.
The facial virus decimated the population of Tasmanian Devils.

Forms of the word: decimated, decimating, decimation

Despondent

1. having lost heart, courage or hope; depressed.

Their house had burnt to the ground and they had managed to save their children but were totally despondent because of the loss of all personal belongings.
At times when you are feeling despondent, you should remind yourself that somebody else was crucified for you on a cross.
Members of the human race who survive on Mars will feel quite despondent about the destruction of planet Earth.

Forms of the word: despondency, despondently

Discretion

1. the power or right of deciding or acting according to one's own judgment.

For the purpose of more efficient government, all Acts of Parliament ought to incorporate a broader element of Ministerial discretion.
Upon learning that a fellow astronaut had been left behind on Mars, the team were granted discretion as to whether or not they returned to save him.

2. the quality of being discreet.

Though one might be best advised to adhere rigidly to rules and regulations most of the time, there are times when one must use one's discretion.

Forms of the word: discretionary

Dissipate

1. to scatter or become scattered in various directions; disperse; disintegrate.

If you lift a manhole lid that hasn't been disturbed for some time you will probably see a profusion of cockroaches dissipate in various directions.
If the Aussie redback spider dissipates into the United States and breeds with the American black widow, will their mutant offspring be able to reproduce?
Some gases do not seem to dissipate to fill an entire area the way they should!

Extraneous

1. introduced or coming from without; not belonging or proper to a thing; external; foreign.

The abiding by community expectation is now an extraneous aspect of the process of government.
Is it really so extraneous to human nature to assist those of humble means in so many countries where children have little or no food to eat?
The requirement of celibacy of its priesthood by the Catholic Church is totally extraneous to fundamental human nature.

Fastidious

1. very particular and careful.

It wasn't what you would call a family restaurant – no, everything was in place and meticulously cleaned by this most fastidious entrepreneur.

She always turned her toaster upside down and emptied her kettle and refilled it with clean water before using them, in case a cockroach had made its way into her utensils, because when it came to food preparation, she was a very fastidious person.
Queen Elizabeth II wore a new gown every day because she was an extremely fastidious monarch, but what happened to her clothes after she had worn them just once?

Improvise

1. to prepare or provide quickly, using the materials at hand.

They were trapped in a snowstorm in the lower reaches of New Zealand's Mount Cook without proper shelter, but were able to improvise by digging an ice hut.
They had already set up their bivouac near the Rees-Dart track when they realised they had no sandfly repellent, but they improvised by lighting a small fire upwind.
The Apollo 13 astronauts were in danger of running short of oxygen but were able to improvise with the few materials they did have.

Forms of the word: improvisation

Inadvertent

1. not paying attention; heedless.

Christopher Columbus set sail from Spain believing he was heading toward Japan, but he inadvertently bumped into the Americas.

2. unintentional.

Though the superannuation levy had been planned to boost savings and stimulate investment, it was a totally inadvertent effect that this vast pool of savings would reduce interest rates and inflation rates so drastically.

Technological innovation emanating from space exploration has inadvertently resulted in several monumental technological advancements flowing through to industry in general.

Forms of the word: inadvertently

Inextricable

1. from which one cannot remove or extricate oneself.

There is an inextricable nexus between education levels and career prospects.

2. not able to be undone, freed, etc.

We have promoted tourism in New Zealand so very well in recent decades that we now have a totally inextricable reliance on an industry that we set out to foster as a supplement to an agricultural-based economy.

3. not able to be put in order or solved.

What normally starts as a relatively inexpensive government funded program responding to a need, soon becomes an industry upon which hundreds of quasi-public servants then become dependent in an inextricable manner for their livelihood.

Forms of the word: inextricably

Overt

1. open to view or knowledge; not concealed or secret.

The police finally decided that the overt presence of marked police cars was less effective in catching speeding drivers than are un-marked cars.
The dominance of the Roman Empire was undoubtedly based on an overt show of force.
Aliens who have come here to save us persist in being covert rather than overt.

Pervasive

1. pervade = to spread its presence, activities, influence, etc., throughout.

Though possums were originally introduced to New Zealand from Australia to establish a fur trade, once they established themselves there, they became a pervasive pest.
One of the more intriguing aspects of modern-day economies is that so-called labour market intervention programs that peddle handouts to employers who engage unemployed people, have become so pervasive while the real problems remain unchallenged.
Those alien spacecraft that NASA astronauts refer to as "bogies" are actually quite pervasive within the stratosphere.

Sectarian

1. of or relating to sects.

The atrocities within cultist sectarian movements at Jonestown in Guyana and at Waco Texas were perpetrated by deviants who overtly brainwashed their followers.
Despite state legislation banning all forms of corporal punishment from state funded schools, a small number of quasi-religious sectarian enclaves persist with education by fear.
The world's problem with terrorism can be attributed to sectarian radicals pursuing their ulterior motives of power, money, violence and rape.

Spurious

1. not real or true; counterfeit.

The vast majority of Hindu people believe there is nothing spurious about their belief that life is a succession of incarnations in which we receive our due karma for the way we live.

It was with some trepidation that the New Zealand biologist touted his spurious hypothesis that Australia's redback spider was not a true blue dinkum Aussie but a derivative of the New Zealand katipo spider, which quite strangely only inhabits old logs on beaches.
This international drive toward free trade could merely be a spurious euphemism for reducing workers' wages to the lowest point.

Susceptible

1. easily affected by something, liable.

In a world where international travel is now so inexpensive, more and more promiscuous people are susceptible to transmittable diseases.
As she had consumed far too much wine, she had rendered herself totally susceptible to his advances.

2. able to be affected easily by emotions; impressionable.

Far too many young people are becoming susceptible to indoctrination by radical people of spurious beliefs.

Vengeance

1. the causing of harm or wrong to someone in return for harm received; revenge.

The businessman succeeded through his own persistence and acumen but then sought justice from those who had defrauded him, purely out of vengeance.

2. the desire to cause such harm.

It is with an unfortunate aspect of marital breakdown that the former partners will too often seek vengeance against their estranged partner, rather than being charitable toward them.

3. (with a vengeance) a. with force or violence; b. to a surprising or unusual degree.

We decided to fight those nasty aliens on Independence Day with a vengeance by delivering a nuclear bomb to their mother ship.

Forms of the word: vengeful

Voracious

1. eager or greedy in some activity.

The voracious charlatan had advertised nationally for franchisees to sell disposable cameras and had ripped off several dozen people.
It is an unfortunate fact of life that so many fields of human endeavour only allow the most voracious people to reach the top.
Retail property developers are notoriously voracious people.

Forms of the word: voraciously, voraciousness, voracity

Chapter 15

Ambiguous

1. open to interpretation; having double meaning; equivocal.

The former United States President, Donald Trump, addressed the European national leaders having made his stupendous stricture that he would put America first, but was subsequently quite ambiguous when questioned over what he actually meant.
The world's worst airline disaster – the collision of two Boeing 747 Jumbo jets at the Canary Islands – might have been caused by ambiguous instructions to both pilots, from the control tower.
Australia's banks are now providing superannuation products with disclosure statements laden with ambiguous clauses, for the purpose of deception.

Forms of the word: ambiguity, ambiguously

Concur

1. to agree.

One thing on which so many people concur is that nurturing innovation is an answer to all economic ills.

2. to act together; cooperate; combine.

The coronavirus had literally forced both major political parties to concur on a range of measures to prevent massive unemployment.

3. to happen at the same time.

The mass destruction of tropical rainforest within the Amazon basin will duly concur with the advent of the next Ice Age.

Forms of the word: concurrence

Converse

1. turned about; opposite or contrary in direction or action (adj.).

In Jesus' parable of the vineyard workers the early starters believed they would be paid more than the late starters but, conversely, they were all given the same reward - eternal life.
Many people enter politics with good intentions but conversely their priority changes to just keeping their bum on their seat.

2. a thing which is the opposite or contrary of another (noun).

If you venture into the Karri forest of Western Australia expecting to find endless square kilometres of pristine old growth forest, you might find that the massive clear-felling of trees means the reality is quite the converse.

Forms of the word: conversely

Crass

1. stupid; gross.

As the footbridge across the Clinton River near Milford Sound was clearly signposted to allow one person only at a time, it was gravely crass for all five trekkers to try to cross at once.
The newly elected Senator was not beyond reproach because, being overtly racist, she was prone to making crass comments about all people who subscribed to beliefs different to her own.
Former President Trump did stand for re-election, but his tendency to make crass racist comments about foreigners brought him down.

Forms of the word: crassly, crassness

Devoid

1. empty of or free from.

People who perpetrate systematic fraud upon others for the sake of their own wealth are totally devoid of integrity.
Gamblers who jeopardise their family's life savings to feed their habit must surely be devoid of any sense of responsibility.
As human beings we must not be devoid of compassion for starving children.

Dogmatic

1. giving opinions without proof and expecting people to accept them.

The United States military establishment had resorted to warning former high-ranking military personnel against touting their dogmatic opinions that aliens are already amongst us.
The re-election of the government had been abetted by dogmatic diehards from the Opposition Left's insistence on a revision of capital gains tax with a view to retrospectivity.
Two of the essential attributes of religious dogmatists are profound ego and malice for other people.

Forms of the word: dogmatical, dogmatically, dogmatism, dogmatist, dogmatise

Futile

1. incapable of producing any result; ineffective.

If aliens do visit us it would be futile to take them on.
It will be entirely futile trying to traverse the universe unless we work out how to travel at the speed of light squared.
Attempting to contrive a rescue plan was an exercise in futility as long as Gilligan was on the island.

Forms of the word: futility

Inception

1. beginning; start.

Since the inception of contraception, the populations of western economies have remained at sustainable levels.
There is no doubt that the inception of the space race realised the expediting of a great number of advances in technology.
Since the inception of the generation of electricity we have utilised machines to do much of our work.

Incongruous

1. out of keeping or place; inappropriate; absurd.

The legal profession had so distorted its priorities away from justice and towards the propagation of its wealth, that its activities had become virtually entirely incongruous with notions of justice.
The fact that Jesus drove the money racketeers from the temple because they were not genuinely people of God seems just a little incongruous with usury televangelists collecting copious amounts of money at their so-called church meetings.
Max Weber's book "The Protestant Ethic and the Spirit of Capitalism" exemplified the incongruity between Protestants and Catholics as industrialists during Europe's Industrial Revolution.

Forms of the word: incongruent, incongruity, incongruously

Insinuate

1. to suggest or hint slyly.

She did not actually state that her husband had sneaked out during the night, but she was able to insinuate to the police that he had.

If you have a troublemaker at work you could comment about them at staff meetings to insinuate that they cause problems, rather than have them cause more problems for you.
In his classical novel "The Power Elite" American sociologist C. Wright Mills did more than merely insinuate the interplay between the corporate rich, the military establishment and Congress.

Forms of the word: insinuated, insinuating, insinuation

Obnoxious

1. objectionable; offensive; odious.

It is because bikies change their underwear so infrequently that they can emit such obnoxious odours when they catch a crowded bus or train.
What made the space shuttle commander even more inclined to eject her off-sider was his tendency, more than others, to emit obnoxious odours in such confined spaces.
The oppression of millions of African people in South Africa for such a prolonged period is one of the most obnoxious situations in human history.

Prerogative

1. an exclusive or established right or privilege belonging to an office, position, or person.

The school principal knew it was entirely his prerogative whether or not to shave his head in support of the cancer foundation but elected to do so as an overt show of support for the students who had done the same.
It is entirely your prerogative whether or not you live your life subscribing to the Golden Rule – to do unto others as you would have them do unto you.
Pope Francis' benevolent comment regarding gay marriage upset his College of Cardinals, but as the Catholic Pontiff it was his prerogative to say whatever he felt to be truth.

Protrude

1. to (cause to) project or stick out.

Some men are born great, some achieve greatness - and some have greatness thrust upon them - meaning that most great men do protrude themselves to have greatness thrust upon them.
Egotistical people will normally endeavour to protrude themselves in one way or another.
Australia's wonder dog - the kelpie - is certainly not averse to protruding itself when it comes to rounding up those mindless sheep.

Forms of the word: protrusive, protrusion

Prudent

1. prudence = careful, practical wisdom; good judgment.

Before going on strike for a petty-minded cause it may be prudent for you to ascertain if it is now legal to do so.
The employer really had no right to ask his employee about the nature of her illness and should have been far more prudent in the way he handled any reference to the employee's prolonged absence.
International diplomacy requires the ultimate in levels of prudence.

Rapacious

1. greedy in a violent and unpleasant way; predatory; extortionate.

Mining companies that had exploited coal and gas reserves for decades continued to downplay the adverse effects on the Earth's climate, as their shareholders were quite rapacious by nature.
Eventually it was because of their rapacity that the greedy retail developers came unstuck because upon expiry of their leases they could not attract replacement tenants.

"God wants you to be wealthy - and how can I preach this if I, myself, am poor?" chanted the rapacious Pentecostal televangelist.

Forms of the word: rapacity

Reprieve

1. to relieve (someone) from impending punishment (verb).

The judicious judge decided to reprieve the juvenile, whose first offence was to steal a candy bar from the supermarket.

2. any rest or temporary relief (noun).

Hopefully our medical researchers can develop a vaccine to provide a reprieve from this COVID-19 virus that has completely changed the world.
The NATO fighters had been in the air when the last-minute reprieve was granted, following fresh assurances from the dictator; but one week later they were in the air again.

Reticent

1. tending to be silent; not inclined to speak freely; reserved.

The sailors had heard of the severe weather warning but remained somewhat reticent due to the status of this internationally renowned yacht race.
Military personnel are required to be reticent even if they do doubt orders from above.
The navy personnel were concerned but remained duly reticent when asked to search for the lost boats within the Bermuda Triangle.

Forms of the word: reticence

Stringent

1. strict; narrowly binding; rigorously exacting.

The employer now had a problem with more than one employee driving whilst intoxicated so she implemented some new stringent regulations.
The crack special air services regiment was not a place for soldiers who were not prepared to tolerate the most stringent requirements.
The holy Shroud of Turin - arguably the burial garment of Jesus Christ - is housed within a vault with stringent security protocols in place.

Forms of the word: stringency, stringently

Temerity

1. foolish boldness; rashness.

After all that she had done to keep her staff in their jobs they one day had the temerity to tell her that she was not a good employer.
The televangelist, in the true spirit of rationalisation, had the temerity to explain that his private golf course was for the purpose of allowing him to experience absolute peace with God, whilst preparing his preaching for the sinners.
The Cardinal had the temerity to suggest that not all victims of sexual abuse were still suffering.

Vanity

1. extreme pride in one's own appearance, qualities, gifts, etc.

So many hopeful young people go to acting school in an attempt to succeed as an actor, partly in pursuit of wealth and fame but perhaps also out of vanity.
The Bhagwan displayed that he was the epitome of vanity by purchasing sixty four Rolls Royce cars for himself, with his followers' money.

2. futility; uselessness.

It would be absolute vanity to expect that Pentecostal televangelists would place the interests of the world's starving children ahead of their own desire for opulence.

Chapter 16

Accentuate

1. to give importance to; emphasise.

In promoting their beautiful country to international tourists, the New Zealand Tourism Commission sought to accentuate the magnificence of New Zealand's rivers and mountains over those of European countries.
In an attempt to make it more difficult for refugees to enter Australia the government decided to accentuate the significance of English skills in the screening process.
Confucius sought to nurture harmony within communities by accentuating the mutual benefits of social cooperation.

Forms of the word: accentuated, accentuating, accentuation

Callous

1. insensitive, hard-hearted.

Our politicians collectively show callous disregard for people whose lives are totally destroyed by fraudsters, retail property developers, insurance companies or banks.
The former Australian Prime Minister's refusal to apologise to the Australian Aboriginal community was a callous display toward their ongoing plight.
What started as just a small flutter at the casino soon became a major problem as she callously frittered away her family's assets.

Forms of the word: callousness

Cognizant

1. cognizance = knowledge; notice.

It is not prudent to venture into the bush in New Zealand on a simple day walk without being cognizant of sudden drastic changes of weather.
It is advisable to remain cognizant of the incidence of king waves when walking on rocks on Western Australia's southern coastline.
Despite the Treaty of Versailles, the British Prime Minister Sir Winston Churchill remained cognizant of the ever-present threat from Nazism.

Conceal

1. to hide; cover or keep from sight.

Drug runners will endeavour to conceal their contraband from authorities in a plethora of innovative ways.

2. to refuse to disclose; keep (something) secret.

Afraid of the mission being dubbed a failure the Russian scientists decided to conceal the fact that their Venus landing module contained a camera, by describing it as a "light contrast detection meter".
Former United States President Barak Obama appeared on the Jimmy Kimmel show and alluded to his government's contact with aliens, but also of the need to conceal this for reasons pertaining to security and to the preservation of social order.

Forms of the word: concealable, concealment

Contentious

1. given to argument.

The role of the United States' Central Intelligence Agency in the overthrow of Chile's socialist President Salvador Allende in 1973 remains one of the most contentious blights between the two nations.

2. characterised by argument.

The Catholic Church acceded to the theory of evolution through Pope Pius XII in 1954 – acknowledging the account of creation in the Bible as metaphorical – thus creating a highly contentious issue within Christianity. Numerous Protestant churches subscribe to Young Earth creationism out of gross ignorance, in defiance of profound scientific knowledge, merely in order to maintain this contentious stance against the Church of Rome.

Forms of the word: contentiously

Delineate

1. to show in words; describe.

If we are going to have federal legislation and state legislation in relation to Aboriginal land rights, it may be necessary to clearly delineate areas of responsibility.
People who are going to sell real estate on Mars need to clearly delineate the areas where there is available water.
The World Health Organization was quick to delineate the areas where people would be most susceptible to the Zika virus.

Forms of the word: delineated, delineating, delineation

Devise

1. to order or arrange a plan of; think out; plan; contrive; invent.

In some work situations, you might get ahead more quickly if you devise more efficient work strategies.
If you go into business with other people, it may be wise to devise a strategy for dissolving the company should somebody start to act irresponsibly.
Karl Marx thought that capitalism would cease to expand, but Karl Benz devised a machine to replace the horse and buggy.

Forms of the word: devised, devising

Discern

1. to see, recognise, or understand clearly.

Most European leaders were able to discern that there was a genuine need to accommodate refugees fleeing from Libya and Iran.
The Kepler telescope is sufficiently powerful to discern planets within the "Goldilocks" habitable zone.

2. to recognise as separate or different; discriminate.

During the Spanish Inquisition, the church failed to discern between genuine alchemists and witches and subsequently burnt all of them at the stake.

Forms of the word: discernible, discerning, discernment

Guile

1. cunning; deceitfulness; treachery.

The Spanish conquistadors displayed considerable guile in befriending the enemy of the Aztec communities in Central America.
Former Libyan dictator Muammar Gaddafi had sufficient guile to arrange that his wife, rather than himself, owned the nation's airline.
Some historians guilefully resorted to misrepresenting the extermination of Tasmania's Aboriginal people by European settlers.

Forms of the word: guileful, guilefully, guileless

Inept

1. not fit or suitable; inappropriate.

It wasn't that the Russian scientists were inept, but there were no guarantees that a camera on the surface of Venus was going to survive long enough in the heat to actually take any pictures at all.

2. awkward or inefficient.

So many transnational corporations pay such little tax because international governments are so inept when it comes to cooperative taxation action.

3. foolish; absurd.

It was surely out of pure ineptitude that we allowed some of our most significant inventions to have to go overseas for venture capital.

Forms of the word: ineptness, ineptitude

Malign

1. to speak ill of; slander (verb).

If you are seeking a good mark in your studies, it might be prudent not to malign your teachers.
In these days of an increasingly litigious minded society, one should be extremely careful about maligning others on a dubious basis.

2. evil in effect; pernicious; baleful (adj.).

The radicalisation of youth toward terrorism for political purposes, made with exhortations to religious beliefs, often stems from the malign influence of self-appointed clerics.

Forms of the word: malignancy, malignant, malignantly

Oblivious

1. forgetful; without remembrance.

He was really in trouble now, for it was the third consecutive year that he had been oblivious to the fact that it was their wedding anniversary.

2. unmindful; unconscious (followed by of or to).

The mining giant knew its mining operations could adversely affect the river system, upon which so many people relied for their livelihood, but it chose to remain oblivious to their situation.
The British settlers seemed to be totally oblivious to the detrimental effects their foxes and rabbits would wreak on the Australian ecology.

Panacea

1. a cure for all diseases, problems, etc.

The corporate sponsorship of inventors is viewed by most people in the community as a panacea of economic ills.
It is not at all surprising that so many large corporations sponsor the space exploration industry, as they see the spinoffs from the world's brains trust as being a panacea of progress.
No doubt the development of the computer spreadsheet heralded a panacea to resolve previously laborious calculations.

Perverse

1. determined or likely to go against what is expected or desired; contrary.

Trade union officials have witnessed the demise of socialism in so many countries, yet many remain so perverse in wanting to steer our working-class party down the road of nationalising industries.

2. turned away from what is right, good, or proper; wicked.

Donald brazenly decided to campaign on a platform of banning Muslim people from entering the United States, but the vast majority of good American citizens saw this for the perverse, racist taunt that it was.
The fact that lawyers encourage their clients to lie under oath before the courts and even before God is regarded by the general community as a total perversion of our institution of law.

Forms of the word: perversely, perversion

Postulate

1. to ask, demand, or claim.

In submitting its triennial stake for funding, NASA would postulate that its scientists desperately needed to research the possibility of anti-gravity motion.

2. to claim or take for granted the existence or truth of, especially as a basis for reasoning.

Scientists at the Laser Interferometer Gravitational-Wave Observatory postulated that they had detected gravitational waves from two merging black holes in September of 2015.
Sir David Attenborough would never relent on postulating the theory of evolution despite death threats being levelled against him by fundamentalist Christians.

Recompense

1. to repay or reward, for service, aid, etc. (verb).

Inveterate car thieves might be sent off to isolated boot camps, but they will never be required to recompense the insurance companies.

2. a repayment made, as for loss, injury, etc. (noun).

The proceeds of crime legislation should be enhanced to allow the government to extend some form of recompense to victims of crime.
The people of England pay the British Royal Family substantial sums of money as recompense for all the wonderful services they provide.

Reprobate

1. an unprincipled, immoral or wicked person (noun).

The first visit to Cuba by a United States President – Mr. Barak Obama - in almost ninety years indicated that Fidel Castro was no longer considered to be a political reprobate.
The sentencing judge duly branded the deviants who left their country to join the forces of terrorists as total reprobates.

2. bad; morally depraved; unprincipled (adj.).

The fact that so many reprobate young people now inflict horrific forms of violence upon elderly citizens is surely a reliable indicator that the strength of social bonding in our community has reached an all-time low.

Forms of the word: reprobation

Tenuous

1. lacking a firm or sound basis; weak; vague; flimsy.

As the Americans were quite adept at various forms of trickery and stealth, the Kiwi's had only a tenuous hold on the America's Cup.
The sale of plots of land on Mars, that some people are selling already, might be just a little tenuous if we don't actually establish a colony there.
Our hold on planet Earth may be rather tenuous if a roaming black hole or a bullet star comes too close to our sun.

Travesty

1. any inferior or distorted likeness or imitation.

The sentencing of the juvenile offenders for the maximum period allowable under the law was a major travesty of justice.

It was a total travesty that the government had initiated a Parliamentary Inquiry rather than a Royal Commission into the problem of Aboriginal deaths in custody.
Once again, the accused murderer's lawyer had instructed him to plead not guilty in a blatant travesty of the concept of justice.

Vitriol

1. something sharp, bitter, or severe, as criticism, speech, etc.

The retired judge dished up a serve of the most fervent vitriol to his counterparts who had adulterated the profession for money.
John Lennon was served a double dose of vitriol from conservative America for stating that the Beatles were probably more popular than Jesus Christ, but they failed to understand that his comment was more an indictment on the Beatles army of young fans.
Sometimes it doesn't hurt somebody who is not pulling their weight to give them a dose of vitriolic criticism.

Forms of the word: vitriolic

Chapter 17

Abject

1. completely miserable; humiliating.

There are so many millions of children who live in abject poverty because as human beings we are unable to feed them.

2. humble; servile.

Mother Teresa of Calcutta lived a totally abject life for the sake of helping the poor.

3. deserving contempt.

The chaos caused by the hurricane gave rise to the most abject, despicable looters rummaging and ransacking through the ruins.

Forms of the word: abjection, abjectness

Amenable

1. willing to listen, take suggestions, etc.; cooperative.

After their defeat in the American Civil War, the Confederate states became far more amenable to the proposal to abolish slavery.
A significant aspect of Australian Aboriginal culture that ensured the survival of kinship systems was that younger persons remained amenable toward their elders.
People who subscribe to the universal law of "do unto others as you would have them do unto you" are far more amenable than those who do not.

Forms of the word: amenability, amenableness, amenably

Appalling

1. appal = to strike with fear; fill with alarm and horror.

The incidence of violence against elderly people was so appalling that one politician postulated that some young people had been trained by adults into terrorist acts against the elderly.
The treatment of slaves by wealthy plantation owners in the southern states of northern America in the 18th and 19th centuries is one of the more appalling chapters in United States history.
The "ice epidemic" has wreaked an appalling cost on both law enforcement and medical services.

Forms of the word: appalled

Attain

1. to reach or complete by continued effort; accomplish; achieve.

We must strive through the United Nations to attain a situation where endemic poverty and starvation will be eradicated from Earth.
It is only through a lot of long distance running and repetitive hard work over shorter distances that middle-distance runners eventually attain the ultimate success - to run a sub-four-minute mile.
It is through adherence to the Great Commandment of Jesus Christ - to "love your neighbour as yourself" - that we will attain the personal qualities that will lead us back to God.

Belligerent

1. warlike; given to fighting or quarrelling.

Though both sides in the cold war had spies in the other's country, there would be no exonerating of spies by belligerent governments.
The countries that had presided over ethnic cleansing had their opportunity to retreat, but out of belligerent mindedness decided to take on the allies at war.

Yet another suicide bombing against innocent civilians demonstrated the belligerent mindset of terrorists who think they should kill people in the name of religion.

Forms of the word: belligerence

Compulsion

1. **the act of forcing; constraint; coercion.**

All nations must feel a profound compulsion to fight terrorism for the sake of future humanity.

2. **the state of being compelled.**

The young doctor from Eastern Europe, realising how fortunate she was to be accepted into Australia, felt a compulsion to "go bush" to serve remote Aboriginal communities.
As a last resort to locating the intrepid wanderer in the desert, the Aboriginal trackers successfully followed their compulsion in searching at the base of the ranges, where water would accumulate.

Forms of the word: compulsive, compulsorily, compulsory

Covert

1. **hidden; secret; disguised.**

Spies from both the United States and the former Soviet Union were engaged in covert operations in the other country.
Those aliens are certainly covert in their observations of our errant superpowers and of their potential for mutual destruction.
The police finally realised that covert surveillance in unmarked patrol cars was the most effective way of keeping hoons off our roads.

Forms of the word: covertly

Elicit

1. to draw or bring out.

The horrendous sentencing of petty criminals in the United States was attributable to the United States government's attempts to elicit civic conformity from its citizens.
The bishop resorted to telling funny stories as he tried in vain to elicit some discussion among the reticent nuns, who seemed too much in awe of his presence to say anything.
Two of the founders of democratic theory Jean Jacques Rousseau and John Stuart Mill endeavoured to elicit greater participation by the people in the process of government.

Forms of the word: elicitation

Emanate

1. to flow or come out; originate.

What should emanate from high school education into belief systems will, hopefully, be greater tolerance, understanding and acceptance of people from a range of cultures, into which they were born and socialised.
The medical profession was concerned of what might emanate from a Parliamentary enquiry into health funding, in terms of disclosing how medical professionals freely access the public purse.
Following the astounding revelations of deep space from the Hubble Telescope, we can only wonder what might eventually emanate from the more powerful James Webb Telescope launched in 2021.

Forms of the word: emanating, emanation

Exonerate

1. to clear of a charge, etc.; free from blame.

He had always protested his innocence and was eventually exonerated when a DNA match implicated an inveterate criminal in the crime.
As a gesture of goodwill, the parties of the protracted conflict agreed to exonerate imprisoned soldiers from both sides, in the hope of going forward together toward a dialogue of peace.
Nobody will ever exonerate the surviving Boston bomber.

Forms of the word: exonerated, exonerating, exoneration

Expound

1. to set forth or state in detail.

As it seemed that his audience did not quite understand what he meant by the cost of foregone opportunity, he was compelled to expound upon his ideas of assessing net benefit in terms of the unknown entities.

2. to explain; interpret.

The instigator of the Disclosure Project, Dr. Steven Greer, was called upon by the Congressional Committee to expound his belief that aliens had established their base on the dark side of the moon.
Sarah went public again to expound upon her fears that Alaska lay between two foreign nations - those being, according to Sarah, Canada and Russia.

Forms of the word: exponent, exposition

Facetious

1. intended to be amusing.

The plaintiff confronted the attorney-general, who was venting his anger at being sued for dereliction of duty, with a barrage of witty, facetious jibes.
The young student, intent upon his own career in education, was well versed in education theory and sought to nark his school teachers with facetious quips about their draconian use of corporal punishment.

The reporter made a facetious comment regarding Sarah's dubious knowledge of geography.

Impetuous

1. acting with or noted for sudden or hasty energy.

On the following hole the golfer missed another short putt, so he impetuously threw his putter and then his caddy into the lake.
International relations between governments are not a place for people who are impetuous, because attributes of tact and diplomacy are imperative.
Sarah was prone to impetuous gaffes, despite being primed by her mentors.

Forms of the word: impetuosity, impetuously

Incense

1. to make angry; enrage.

The children knew their mother would be angry that they had by painted on the wall, but their use of insoluble paint only served to incense her.
The local police were terribly concerned about the group of tourists trekking into the Great Sandy Desert and had reason to be incensed by suggestions that the search effort was being conducted in a cursory manner.
The Pontiff's comments that the church would reconsider its doctrine regarding de facto marriages would incense his College of Cardinals.

Forms of the word: incensed, incensing

Induce

1. to lead or move by persuasion or influence to some action, state of mind, etc.

You can usually induce kids to be well behaved with a promise of good Christmas presents.
The renegade dictator offered six billion dollars of his nation's wealth to induce any country to provide himself and his aides with safety in exile.
He was loathed by the establishment, but the lyrics of one James Douglas Morrison did induce a generation of young people to revolt against the war in Vietnam.

Forms of the word: induced, inducing, inducement

Obstinate

1. firmly and often stupidly keeping to one's purpose, opinion, etc.

The rather obtuse former Australian Prime Minister was totally obstinate in his stance, that global warming treaties would not cost Australians any jobs.
Despite the NASA Lunar Orbiter clearly depicting images of the Apollo landing sites, some conspiracy theorists obstinately persist with their claims.
That person who thought that north was south actually spent the night in the wilderness because, being so obstinate, he did go in the opposite direction.

Forms of the word: obstinacy, obstinately

Proclivity

1. a natural or habitual inclination or tendency; propensity; predisposition.

The parameters of the small business environment were changing, as there were now so many people with a proclivity for making a quick buck at the expenses of somebody else, that the unwary would be skinned one way or another.
This so-called Islamic State terrorist group is totally comprised of people with a distinct and profound proclivity toward violence.

The insurance ombudsman's office was laden with former insurance industry staff with a distinct proclivity toward protecting insurers.

Protagonist

1. any leading character in the support of a movement, cause, etc.

There were now vast numbers of people following the protagonist in pursuit of justice against the errant government for its negligence.
It was because of her indelible belief that our forests belong to everybody that the high-profile protagonist of preservation was pleased to be arrested for chaining herself to a bulldozer.
The great Mohandas Gandhi was the main protagonist for a peaceful movement for independence from Britain.

Ramify

1. to divide or spread out into branches or branch-like parts.

If you treat just one of your customers with indifference or contempt do not be surprised if the consequences for your business ramify somewhat.
It was so totally inept for politicians to fail to acknowledge the ramifications of allowing people who engaged in criminal activity to permeate their way to the top in small business.
Our community of metaphysical scientists is overwhelmingly excited about the ramifications of the discovery of gravitational waves.

Forms of the word: ramified, ramifying

Resilient

1. readily recovering, especially from sickness, depression, etc.; buoyant; cheerful.

Yes, the cane toad is such a resilient character that we may all have to develop a liking for French cuisine.
Despite their claims that the trekker was a particularly resilient character, it was known that even Aboriginal people had perished in the desert without adequate protection.
The United States flagship, USS Enterprise, was damaged several times during World War II, but her resilience saw her intact when the conflict ended.

Forms of the word: resilience, resiliency

Chapter 18

Affinity

1. a natural liking for, or attraction to, a person or thing.

In their spiritual belief systems, Australia's Aboriginal people have developed an inextricable affinity with their land that non-Aboriginal people find difficult to understand.
Aspiring students of veterinary science must display an affinity towards all types of animals.
Domestic dogs have been selectively bred by humans from the grey wolf, but they now have a natural affinity toward loving people.

Forms of the word: affinitive

Alleviate

1. to make (pain, punishment, etc.) easier to be accepted; lessen; mitigate.

Aid organisations such as the Catholic Mission and World Vision do so much in an effort to alleviate poverty in underdeveloped countries, but they are always in need of additional support.
The philanthropists mooted the idea of providing free telephones to African nations in an attempt to alleviate the endemic poverty that prevails.
We could do so much more to alleviate the suffering of people in third world countries if we did not live in such opulence ourselves.

Forms of the word: alleviated, alleviating, alleviation

Debase

1. reduce in quality; adulterate.

In failing to deliver that apology, the former Prime Minister of Australia was prepared to debase our nation's reputation regarding its relationship with indigenous people.
The atrocities perpetrated by the so-called Islamic State terrorist group will only serve to debase the good name of Islam in the eyes of many non-Islamic people.
It seems that perhaps a majority of criminal legal practitioners are prepared to debase the institution of law by knowingly protecting people who are guilty of serious crime.

Forms of the word: debased, debasing, debasement

Decadence

1. the act or process of falling into a lower state; decay; deterioration.

So many of the social norms that prevail in middle eastern countries, that prevent women from attaining equal rights to men, are so fraught with decadence as to be totally draconian.
It really does go over the heads of most conservative religious leaders that the particular subculture of their churches is viewed as being grossly decadent to normal everyday people.
There is still an abundance of decadent law persisting within legislation that was enacted centuries ago.

Forms of the word: decadency, decadent

Encroach

1. to advance beyond proper limits.

That cane toad has now decided to encroach upon the other Australian states as well, as it seems to have a lot in common with other pests from Queensland.

It might be advisable to stay out of business if you intend to encroach upon the trading area of an established competitor who has the capacity to undercut your prices.
The Russian military had once again decided to encroach upon a former Soviet nation's sovereignty.

Forms of the word: encroachment

Extol

1. to praise highly; laud; eulogize.

It is conventional practice for the best man to extol the virtues of the bride and the groom during his reception speech.
The first man to set foot upon the moon was humbled by the experience and did not fail to extol the scientists and engineers who were responsible for the mission.
It is expected that Members of Congress and parliamentarians will extol the virtues of their fellow deceased, whatever their virtues, or otherwise, might have been.

Exude

1. to come or send out gradually in drops like sweat through pores or small openings.

The former Governor General of Australia was tending to exude a rather alcoholic stench as he opened proceedings for the presentation of the Melbourne Cup.
The young lawyer had been presented with such an armoury of prosecution questions by this new litigation preparation corporation, that he could not help but exude confidence as he strode into court for the trial.
The participants in "Married at First Sight" did exude some confidence to begin with, but reality soon caught up with them.

Forms of the word: exuded, exuding

Fortitude

1. patient courage in times of sickness, hardship, etc.; moral strength.

It was only out of immense fortitude that one man embarked on a course to bring the negligent government before the courts, for failing to provide adequate protection to the people.
The astronauts were all well aware that no rescue missions could be instigated but took their risks with great fortitude.
Despite learning of her husband's philandering, the princess continued her charity work with considerable fortitude.

Furtive

1. sly; shifty.

The vehicle manufacturers were finally required to face the music before a sceptical media that some models were made so easy to steal, that it was regarded as a furtive way of increasing replacement sales.
The young lawyer was fresh enough to challenge the legal fraternity with her idyllic views, implementing her strategy of contingent litigation finance, but had to do so in a rather furtive manner by purchasing shares in the plaintiff corporations.
Through their so-called property council, the retail property developers had furtively conspired to increase rents by more than three hundred percent over a period of just five years.

Impeccable

1. faultless.

He was unanimously elected to the presidency of the law society because he had an absolutely impeccable record in cooking the books.
Whilst many of the champion athletes around him were failing drug detection tests, the three times Olympic champion stood on his impeccable record as a true athlete.
Queen Elizabeth II's reign surpassed that of Queen Victoria's - and she had maintained an impeccable record as the British monarch.

Forms of the word: impeccability

Incarcerate

1. to imprison; confine.

The United States would incarcerate the surviving Boston bomber for life, with never a prospect of being released from jail.
The Bhagwan and his off-sider, Ma Sheila, were now incarcerated in abject prison poverty, but it was clearly a case of "tough titties" - to quote Ma Sheila - that they could not have a Rolls Royce or two in there with them..

2. to enclose; constrict closely.

The entire population of North Korea is literally incarcerated by an oppressive regime of murderous military dictators and their supreme leader puppet.

Forms of the word: incarcerated, incarcerating, incarceration

Invoke

1. to call for with earnest desire.

The President of the United States eventually saw the light and called a press conference to invoke Europe's leaders to put more troops on the ground against the terrorists.

2. to appeal to, as for confirmation.

The former Chancellor of Germany Angela Merkel had addressed her nation to invoke their deep-rooted sentiments against murderous aggressors - such as the so-called Islamic State.

3. to put into effect.

After the British Prime Minister and the French President gave their support to the concept of ground warfare against the so-called Islamic State, NATO decided to invoke a resolution that was tantamount to a declaration of war.

4. to call forth or upon (a spirit) by incantation; conjure.

In the process of providing a spiritual reading, clairvoyant people typically invoke contact with the deceased ancestors of their clients.

Forms of the word: invoked, invoking

Nebulous

1. unclear, vague or confused.

There was something quite nebulous about the detail of the contract that the finance broker was presenting to the elderly investors.
There was nothing nebulous about former United States President Donald Trump's exhortations to the January 6th 2021 rioters, prior to their storming the Capitol Building.
When Edwin Hubble used his new powerful telescope to peer into a rather nebulous looking cloud in the night sky, he was totally enthralled to find it was actually the Andromeda Galaxy.

Pensive

1. deeply, seriously, or sadly thoughtful.

Having lost everything they had worked to accumulate for so long, to her callous husband's compulsive gambling, she sat for the last time on the front steps of her house in a reflective, pensive mood.

It was late in the afternoon when their tent was washed away in one of New Zealand's more volatile rivers, forcing them to ponder the cold night ahead with a pensive concern.
Despite the recent spate of terrorist atrocities the American people are once again feeling rather pensive about sending their sons to war.

Pertain

1. to have reference or relation; relate.

The judge ordered that defence counsel refrain from presenting the medical document about the plaintiff's husband, as such matters did not pertain to the case.
One of the strangest aspects of human nature is how so many people caught red-handed in using drugs to enhance their performance in the sporting arena, can so blatantly lie about their use of drugs for reasons conceivably pertaining only to money.
The prominent French sociologist, Emile Durkheim, wrote his classical work "Suicide" to demonstrate how suicide rates within societies pertain to the strength of social bonds.

Forms of the word: pertaining

Propensity

1. a natural or habitual tendency or inclination.

There is a distinct propensity among televangelists to bring all aspects of Christian life down to financial support for the church, with tithings.
With more than two hundred approved patents, outstanding inventor Thomas Edison had a profound propensity for thinking outside the square.
With such few Federal referenda, we have a propensity for accepting government that is seriously out dated, in an age when progressive mindedness is required to meet the challenges of the future.

Remiss

1. **careless in duty, business, etc.; negligent.**

It was obviously so gravely remiss of the former United States President to share secrets about his nation's submarines, with anybody.
It was so hypocritically remiss of the President's wife to rebuke her husband for his infidelity when she, herself, had been indulging in some of the same.
It is remiss of successive governments for failing to educate Australian farmers that daylight saving does not deny other countries from enjoying their share of sunlight.

Forms of the word: remissness

Sarcastic

1. **Sarcasm = an ironical taunt or jibe; a sneering or cutting remark.**

He told his extremely vain wife that she was one of the most beautiful women he had ever seen and, though he was being sarcastic, his comment was in order to placate her.
The coach said his players gave their all, but it was a sarcastic comment meant to humiliate them after their crushing defeat.
We did say that to put Tasmanian bees into a refrigerator to slow them down would simply, speed them up - but we were being just a tad sarcastic.

Subscribe

1. **to agree, especially by signing one's name.**

If you want young people to live a spiritual life you need to have something quite intelligible for them to subscribe to.
Allow me to subscribe to the view that the litmus test for humanity is whether good people preside over people of wrongdoing.
Though many Protestant American churches still subscribe to Young Earth creationism, believing everything was created approximately six thousand

years ago, the Catholic Church now subscribes to Old Earth creationism, believing that almighty God probably created at the time of the Big Bang.

Vindicate

1. to show to be right or just; justify.

She knew that the profits she would recoup from building the water slide down the mountain would vindicate her decision to invest her money in this extraordinary venture.
There is no doubt that the spinoff to industry from the technology of space exploration vindicates the cost.

2. to support, or defend (a right, cause, etc.) against opposition.

The Democratic candidate was intent on vindicating her immigration policy with exhortations to compassion and charity in the debate against the renegade racist Republican candidate.

Forms of the word: vindication

Chapter 19

Acquiesce

1. to agree, especially in a quiet way; consent.

It was only after considerable scientific and technical representation regarding fire blight, that the Australian agricultural authorities eventually decided to acquiesce to New Zealand to allow the import of apples.
Following track demonstrations that proved the Australian made Ford Falcon was far superior to the American models, Dearborn acquiesced to accepting the design engineering developed in Australia.
Though dozens of soldiers had been killed by their own, the military establishment sought to gain the acquiescence of the rank and file to refer to this as "friendly fire".

Forms of the word: acquiesced, acquiescence, acquiescing, acquiescent

Aspersions

1. a damaging remark or criticism.

Despite having such derogatory aspersions cast upon her, the young attorney persisted in providing an alternative arrangement to the contingency plans now made available through law firms.
Leaders from all parties sought to cast aspersions upon their independent President but the people stood firmly behind their first President of such immense rectitude.
Donald had resorted to a new low by spruiking aspersions regarding alleged infidelity of his main political rival and by seemingly inciting the gun lobby to take action of its own.

Audacity

1. boldness or daring, especially careless boldness.

Those aliens at Area 51 had the audacity to inform former United States President Dwight Eisenhower that the United States government had no jurisdiction there.
The Presidential candidate had the audacity to suggest that the children at the school would still be alive if they had carried their own guns to school.

2. cheek; effrontery; insolence.

The Prime Minister of the developing nation had the audacity to excoriate his fellow neighbouring Prime Minister, who had candidly cited the nexus between aid funding and the oppression of human rights.

Forms of the word: audacious

Commensurate

1. having the same measure or size.

Some notorious governments are duly embarrassed before the United Nations General Assembly to an extent commensurate with their record of violations of the basic human rights of their own citizens.
The Buddha mooted the concept that a succession of incarnations would end in being reunited with God when the amount of devotion, loyalty, charity, honesty and love that you give to others, is more than commensurate with what you receive.
The United States judiciary is notorious for handing down extreme sentences that are clearly not commensurate with the nature of the crime.

Forms of the word: commensurable

Complicity

1. the state of being a partner (in wrongdoing).

There seems to be a distinct degree of complicity within the walls of the United Nations between governments that oppress minority groups.
Some of the best athletes are usually egged on with drug abuse, by their trainers, who by virtue of their complicity are just as reprehensible.
Officially, lawyers who implore their clients to be untruthful before the courts will never be regarded as complicit in their clients' perjury.

Defunct

1. no longer in use; not operative.

The concept of advocates immunity – that protects legal practitioners from claims of negligence for court work – has been rendered defunct in most civilised nations, so why not in Australia?
Surely it is time for the Catholic Church to recognise that the requirement of celibacy from its clergy ought to be banished to oblivion, together with a number of other such defunct practices.
Given the dissolution of the former Soviet Union, the re-unification of the German nation and the integration of communist China into the world economy, it must be time for sociologists to acknowledge that Marxian theory is somewhat defunct.

Denigrate

1. to devalue the importance or worth of; defame.

A former Australian Liberal Party Senator used his parliamentary privilege to label Aboriginal people as "the lowest colour on the civilisation spectrum", in a blatant attempt to denigrate this very meek race of people.
The Opposition referred to his conviction of bashing an Aboriginal person with an iron bar, in a justifiable effort to denigrate the defunct Senator.

The Royal Commission into union corruption instigated by the Liberal Party government, was clearly an attempt to denigrate the reputation of workers' unions, purely for political advantage.

Forms of the word: denigrated, denigrating, denigration, denigrator

Derogatory

1. showing or causing lack of respect; disparaging; depreciatory.

One might be best advised to be circumspect about making derogatory remarks about one's employer, spouse or family.
People with a chip on their shoulder or a bee under their bonnet have a proclivity towards making derogatory comments about other people.
Despite the fact that the Australian Constitution forbids the Australian Federal Parliament from legislating on grounds pertaining to religion, there is no paucity of ignoramuses making derogatory comments about immigration policy.

Forms of the word: derogative

Enigma

1. somebody or something puzzling or unable to be explained.

The great enigma facing modern day ecumenical religious groups is how to accommodate the extreme fundamentalists – particularly Christian and Muslim fundamentalists - and all the problems they cause, within God's church on earth.
One of the most enigmatic questions that still puzzles NASA today, is the origin of the spacecraft that the Apollo 11 astronauts saw outside their window if the final stage of Apollo 11, the S-IVB, was more than 6,000 miles away.
Despite most sightings of UFO's being explicable, there is a small percentage that still poses a real enigma to the military and to science.

Forms of the word: enigmatic, enigmatically

Euphemism

1. a mild word or phrase chosen to replace one that is more direct but less pleasant.

Some fundamentalist sects have specialised in responding to questions - that might expose them for their bigotry - with various forms of euphemism.
Property developers brought before the courts to answer accusations of double charging "variable outgoing" costs against different groups of tenants, are likely to answer specific questions in a euphemistic manner.
The superannuation fund managers had colluded to devise product disclosure statements that concealed nightmare clauses with euphemistic semantics.

Forms of the word: euphemistic, euphemistically

Ignominy

1. disgrace; dishonour; public contempt.

The historical recording of the actions of some of the more infamous cult heroes, such as Charles Taze Russell and Joseph Smith, has progressed to the point where they are treated ignominiously by all encyclopaedia.
The champion full forward was playing his last game and rather than bowing out gracefully, he resorted to instigating a bit of a punch up with the full back in what became an ignominious and inglorious exit.
The former Australian cricket captain had to live the rest of his life suffering the ignominy of instigating that grubber against our closest friends - the Kiwis.

Forms of the word: ignominious

Infringe

1. to break, as a rule; violate or transgress.

Driving your car in a restricted school zone may result in you receiving a fine if you infringe the speed limits.
The mining company decided to proceed with drilling exploration despite not having received approval from the indigenous landowners, but in doing so it infringed a court order.

2. to move in, encroach or trespass.

There may be a good case for tucking your trouser legs into your socks if you decide to infringe upon the territory of a colony of sergeant bull ants.

Insular

1. of or related to an island or islands.

The musicians in the symphony orchestra had developed into a core group of friends who socialised every weekend, but failed to realise how insular they had become from the general community of young people.
The Branch Davidian sect and the Heaven's Gate sect of religious fundamentalists had each established their own compound out of town, because they were extremely insular communities.

2. narrow minded.

Dogmatic religious fundamentalists who subscribe only to their own beliefs are so insular that they fail to realise the almighty deity who created the universe would be a God of infinite compassion, mercy and love.

Nonchalant

1. coolly unconcerned, indifferent; casual.

Those dentists can stick a needle in your gum when they give you an injection and seem so nonchalant about the pain they cause.

Perhaps we will all be rather less nonchalant about our universe if our metaphysical scientists can crack the enigmatic code of space/time travel. James Douglas Morrison of Doors fame might have seemed a little nonchalant about the soldiers pointing guns at him through his limousine window, but he was probably drunk.

Plethora

1. overfullness; overabundance.

As one of the seven natural wonders of the world, Queensland's Great Barrier Reef is teeming with a plethora of diverse marine life.
People of goodwill who make it their personal mission in life to address the problems caused by nefarious people, will probably need to venture into a plethora of areas of commercial activity.
Investigators looking into the activities of bankers who caused the global financial crisis found a plethora of transgressions from legal banking protocols.

Rationalise

1. to justify one's behaviour by apparently sensible explanations, to deceive oneself or others.

It was something of a foible that the renegade dictator would stash so much of his country's wealth away for himself, but he was able to rationalise this with his references to the United States being the real enemy of his people.
Political terrorists rationalise their true motives - power, money, violence and rape - with their exhortations to Islam.
A typical televangelist will have no problem rationalising their accumulation of wealth, by telling their followers that God wants them all to be wealthy.

Rebuke

1. a scolding; reprimand (noun).

The United Nations has now attained such a level of repute in terms of international diplomacy, that any form of rebuke from the United Nations towards one's country is regarded as a major international embarrassment.
The farmer who wanted a wife came in for considerable rebuke from the women's magazines, for choosing Rebecca rather than Chantelle.

2. to scold; reprove (verb).

The professor of sociology who specialised in religious belief systems and was called upon by the television network following the arrival of a UFO in New York City, delivered her rebuke of dogmatic Christian churches that would experience total bewilderment from such an event.

Receptive

1. having the quality of receiving or taking in.

Fundamentalist Protestant preachers need to be more receptive to the Catholic doctrine espoused as "the anonymous Christian" - that almighty God does not require a person to be an overt Christian to attain eternal life.

2. able or quick to receive ideas, suggestions, etc.

A smart business person will always be receptive to listening intently to complaints from customers.
Those farmers and their aspiring wives are all just a little too receptive to a precipitant marriage.

Forms of the word: receptivity, receptiveness

Relinquish

1. to give up, put aside, or surrender (a possession, right, plan, hope, etc.).

As a sovereign people we ought not relinquish our right to elect our own President.
Renegade dictators who entrench themselves in power with blatant propaganda never relinquish their hold on power because they usually make a fortune from deceiving their people.
The legal fraternity in Australia is the last to relinquish the abomination of advocates' immunity, meaning Australian citizens cannot successfully sue their lawyer if they botch-up their case in court.

Subjugate

1. to bring under complete control or into subjection; subdue; conquer.

It is typical for cult leaders to subjugate their subjects through fear of retribution by God.
This draconian education philosophy was supposedly based on discipline and respect for authority but, in reality, it was little more than total subjugation of students.
The North Korean dictatorship completely subjugates the vast majority of its people, who are subjected to a life of abject poverty.

Forms of the word: subjugated, subjugating, subjugation

Chapter 20

Acrimonious

1. sharpness, harshness or bitterness of temper or speech.

Vehemently criticising other people for their beliefs rather than nurturing an environment of education and understanding can only lead to acrimonious attitudes within our community.
The accusations against some cyclists in the race only gave rise to considerable acrimony between them and officials because the cyclists knew that other teams were past their eyeballs on drugs also.
The acrimony that existed between neighbouring countries Iran and Iraq for such a long time resulted in an eight year war.

Ameliorate

1. to make or become better; improve.

We should attempt to ameliorate the atrocious situation of crime against elderly citizens by involving some elderly people in youth corrective programs.
The only way to ameliorate the situation of drugs dominating sport is to extend the level of independent monitoring in between major sporting events.
The passing of legislation to legalise the medicinal use of some recreational drugs will ameliorate the quality of life of many people who are inflicted with various diseases.

Forms of the word: ameliorated, ameliorating, amelioration

Castigate

1. to punish in order to correct; criticise.

Just one more missed putt and that irascible tournament golfer would severely castigate his already saturated caddy.
The secretary of the Defence Department was severely castigated by the Minister for presiding over a submarine project that was fraught with so many problems.
If Martin Luther were here today, he would scathingly castigate Protestant preachers for their money racketeering.

Forms of the word: castigated, castigating, castigation

Depict

1. to represent in words; describe.

Surely the future of religious veneration, in a new millennium of the blending of western rationalism with eastern philosophies, will depict the essence of the great teachers, such as Jesus, Confucius, Muhammad and the Buddha.
There is an absolutely imperative need for our secondary education systems to extend values education even further into personality psychology, to depict those character traits that might be assumed by the community as desirable rather than undesirable.
Parkinson's Law - that "work expands to occupy the maximum allowable time to achieve its completion" - is a euphemistic depiction that lazy people will take that long if you allow them to.

Forms of the word: depiction

Diligent

1. constant and careful in doing something.

As she was such a diligent worker she maintained an ongoing list of work commitments that she prioritised and updated on a daily basis.

In a world now dominated by the privatisation of government functions and diminished tolerance of employees who are not dollar effective, only the most diligent workers can expect security in employment.

2. done with careful attention; painstaking.

The purchaser of the café sued his own accountant for his lack of due diligence in analysing the trading figures.

Forms of the word: diligence

Disdain

1. to look down on or treat as lesser, despise; scorn (verb).

Yes we should regard all door-knocking peddlers of religious fringe belief systems of spurious doctrine with disdain.

2. a feeling of contempt for anything regarded as unworthy; scorn (noun).

The world community should regard the enormous expense on military hardware with considerable disdain.
The law society's insurance company had a notorious reputation for treating claimants with the utmost disdain.

Forms of the word: disdainful, disdainfully

Diverge

1. to move or lie in different directions from a common point; branch off.

On a rectangular map of the world the longitudinal meridian diverge so that they are depicted as being parallel to each other whereas, in reality, they converge at the poles.

Sections of a river that has constructed a delta near the ocean diverge away from each other as they approach the river mouth.
The farmer explained to the “farmer wants a wife” contestant that it was time for their friendship to take a course of divergence.

Epitomise

1. a representation or typical example of something.

Pope John the twenty-third epitomised the modern day effort of ecumenism and integration of mainstream Christian beliefs.
Some doctors who still have their patients' health as the reason for practicing epitomise what medicine used to be about.
With his famous stricture of "whoever has done this, you're gonna hear us" former United States President George W. Bush epitomised the feeling of all American people at that time.

Forms of the word: epitome

Fervent

1. very warm and earnest in feeling; ardent.

Those who advocate integration into a multicultural society usually become quite fervent in the face of racism, bigotry and intolerance.
Being somewhat imbibed with a sense of location within the history of the human race, the successful billionaire became the most fervent supporter of World Vision's campaign to save starving children.
The great Chinese philosopher Confucius was a fervent believer that the social bonding that prevails within a family could be extrapolated to the wider community to engender social cooperation rather than conflict.

Forms of the word: fervently, ferventness

Imbue

1. to soak or fill, as with feelings, opinions, etc.

To create a better future for the entire world we ought to do our utmost to imbue our young people with a sense of co-operation toward countries beset with famine.
The people shall coalesce towards extirpating politicians who fail to imbue us with concepts and notions directed towards ameliorating our society.
Jesus gave his disciples the parable of "The Prodigal Son" to imbue them with a willingness to forgive others.

Forms of the word: imbued, imbuing

Incessant

1. continuing without stopping.

The bane of modern day intelligentsia is this incessant carping criticism of ethnic groups, by persons not suitably disposed to decision making for the entire community.
Nobody on the bus from Mount Cook to Dunedin wanted to sit next to the American because of his incessant comparing of geographical features with similar features in his own country.
Army ants go about their day on the forest floor with incessant ravaging, but they do play an important role within the total ecology.

Insidious

1. intended to trap or deceive.

The radicalisation of young people by extremists who purport to be religious has become an insidious strategy of modern terrorism.

2. secretly deceitful.

Further development of gas and coal reserves will simply exacerbate the insidious buildup of carbon dioxide in planet Earth's atmosphere.

3. operating unnoticed but with serious effect.

It has been the insidious way that drugs have slowly crept into sport over a period of decades that have made it so difficult for any would-be honest athletes to be competitive.

Forms of the word: insidiously

Nefarious

1. very wicked; iniquitous.

The utterances of people who espouse equality as meaning the abolition of equity programs that enhance people who are disadvantaged, many from birth, must be exposed for their nefarious intentions.
So many athletes caught up in the drugs merry-go-round are actually victims of their managers and their nefarious attempts to make a lot of money from sport for themselves.
Despite the Chinese nation successfully integrating into the economic world, there are still some prevailing nefarious communist traits that subjugate people's freedom.

Perpetuate

1. continuing or enduring forever or indefinitely.

Fundamentalist Christian churches claim to believe in the Holy Bible as a way of perpetuating their belief that only Christians can be granted eternal life.
The politicians resorted to using the cash rate, rather than indirect taxes, to control inflation to perpetuate the prevailing situation where mortgage holders paid an enormous price - rather than everybody paying something.
Unfortunately for Marxian theorists, modern day economic reality means that communism could not be perpetuated due to the prohibitive cost of control -

there being a politician, a bureaucrat, a police officer and a soldier for every ten citizens.

Petulant

1. moved to or showing sudden, inpatient annoyance, especially over some unimportant thing or event, etc.

Those petulant minded, inimical racists must be extirpated from public life by people of goodwill.
One could not blame the Secretary of Defence for being a little petulant in his responses to the tribunal, as his unfair dismissal was a classic case of finding a scapegoat.
The footballer had been scrubbed for abusing the umpire, which was not surprising given his petulant nature.

Forms of the word: petulance

Reprisal

1. hurt or damage caused to (a person, army, etc.) in return for damage received; retaliation.

The invading country had been forced to withdraw from its neighbour's land but set fire to all their oil wells as a form of reprisal.
One of the worst things you can do in a marriage is resort to some form of reprisal if your partner does something wrong that hurts you.
The Boston Tea Party was reputedly a form of reprisal against the imposition of taxes by the British.

Sordid

1. dirty or filthy; squalid.

The United States Presidential campaign had reached a new low with nominees making sordid comments about their opponents' private lives.

2. morally mean; ignoble.

There will be no place in the fostering of our role as an international leader of human rights for sordid bickering over foreign aid programs.
Some wealthy people become so obsessed with the growth of their bank accounts that their parsimonious money laundering nurtures a blatantly sordid disposition toward other people.

Forms of the word: sordidly, sordidness

Specious

1. seemingly good or right but without real worth; superficially pleasing.

The utterances of people who blame our participation in the elevating of less fortunate countries towards prosperity for our own domestic ills, must be exposed for the specious attitude that it is.
The politicians seemed peculiarly unanimous in their support for a goods and services tax, which led a cynical electorate to believe the assurances of greater fairness and equity to be a specious excuse for the politicians gaining more for themselves.
There are so many supposed charitable organisations that usurp too great a proportion of revenues for administration and for remunerating top level executives that their publicised good works are a specious example of deception.

Forms of the word: speciously, speciousness

Stipulate

1. to make a stated demand or arrangement as a condition of agreement.

We must use our position of economic strength to stipulate that other countries within our region address their problems pertaining to human rights.
The Department of Defence had actually failed to stipulate that the submarine computer systems would have to be more sophisticated than Nintendo.
The Chinese government had no choice but to relent because of population demographics and to stipulate that married couples should have two babies rather than one.

Forms of the word: stipulated, stipulating, stipulation

Trepidation

1. fearful alarm or agitation.

It would be with considerable trepidation that we would ever abandon the plight of our less fortunate neighbours.
Some countries are already planning a crewed flight to Mars using ion propulsion, but it would be with considerable trepidation that an astronaut would volunteer for a mission that would be devoid of any rescue plans.
Many Christchurch residents are now feeling some trepidation regarding whether or not they stay in this earthquake prone city - or move.

Chapter 21

Collusion

1. a secret agreement for the purpose of deceiving or doing wrong; conspiracy.

During New Zealand's drought, the truckers delivered water to the Good Old Bastards brewery before the Greymouth Hospital after there had been some collusion with the local hotels and drinkers.
The so-called property council is now bestowing annual awards for the design of new buildings, but the council is really just a smokescreen for blatant collusion to fix rents at exorbitant levels.
The government of Pakistan denied that there had been any collusion in harbouring Osama Bin Laden.

Forms of the word: collusive

Conjecture

1. the formation or expression of an opinion without enough information.

Until the arrival of the UFO in New York City, the United States government had officially persisted with its line that the vast number of claimed sightings left the entire subject of whether aliens had visited Earth, as a matter of complete conjecture.
The scientists expounded their view that the fossilised microbes were an integral part of the rock before it landed on Earth from Mars, but the evidence left much to conjecture.
One metaphysical scientist hypothesised that gravitational waves might travel at the speed of light squared in every conceivable direction simultaneously, but until he produced his mathematics this was pure conjecture.

Culpable

1. deserving blame.

Despite vehement denials from the Pakistani government, the United States regarded it as culpable in its harbouring of terrorists.
It was clearly evident to all rational thinking people in the community that previous governments were culpable for allowing so many people to become dependent upon the forestry industry for their livelihood.
The question remains as to who is culpable for the dissemination of Australia's notorious redback spider into Japan and Germany.

Forms of the word: culpability, culpably

Debilitate

1. to make weak; weaken; enfeeble.

The ongoing war against misguided and brainwashed terrorists, who errantly believe that all non-Islamic westerners are infidel, will never debilitate the free world's resolve to continue fighting.
All the victims of the hospital drug substitution scandal had testified that the poisonous injections had a totally debilitating effect on their daily life.
If the Aussie redback spider makes its way into the United States it will have a debilitating effect on the American black widow spider – by eating it!

Forms of the word: debilitated, debilitating, debilitation

Dissension

1. a difference in opinion; disagreement, especially violent.

There was not a trace of dissension among the participating nations that the President of FIFA had to go.
There was absolutely no dissension within the United Nations that the totally barbaric so-called Islamic State terrorist group had to be defeated at any cost.

There will be considerable dissension among conservative political parties such as the United States Republicans and Australia's Liberal Party over the introduction of a wealth tax because those parties are supported by very wealthy people.

Forms of the word: dissent, dissenter, dissenting

Enmity

1. **the feeling or condition of being hostile; antagonism; animosity.**

Despite the United States of America displaying a long history as a nation of peaceful rectitude, there continues to be considerable enmity within the Russian bureaucracy that festers over into the minds of successive middle eastern autocrats.
There was no dearth of enmity between the British and the French during the American War of Independence.
Many Navajo people justifiably still feel some degree of enmity toward the United States government for subjecting their ancestors to the "Long Walk" of 1864.

Extricate

1. **to free; disengage; disentangle.**

After so many years of owning nothing, she was able to extricate herself from debt by working on a mine site that was free of drugs and alcohol.
Harry Houdini was able to extricate himself from any situation of entrapment.
Far too many women take too long to extricate themselves from being subjected to domestic violence.

Flippant

1. marked by shallow or disrespectful levity (lack of proper seriousness).

Western governments have become so flippant about their massive deficit blowouts that will impact adversely on future generations, when a simple wealth tax would solve the problem.
People who drink heavily and drive motor cars are totally flippant about the possible horrific consequences.
Too many of our world's leaders have spoken flippantly about the melting sea ice at the North Pole.

Forms of the word: flippancy, flippantly

Heinous

1. hateful; odious; gravely reprehensible.

The "Butcher of Bosnia", Ratko Mladic, was sentenced to life in prison for his role in the most heinous slaughter of thousands of Muslim men and boys in Srebrenica in July 1995.
Mao Tse-tung and Joseph Stalin are remembered by millions of fellow compatriots as tyrants responsible for heinous brutality and the deaths of millions of people.
In recent times the world has been aghast at the heinous atrocities perpetrated by terrorists in beheading innocent people.

Incriminate

1. to imply or provide evidence of the crime or fault of (someone).

The discovery of mass graves containing the remains of hundreds of men and boys was sufficient to incriminate Ratko Mladic.
The Senate inquiry found that the incidence of cross referral and dual ownership of specialist services by medical practitioners to be the most

incriminating aspect of the alleged factitious contrivance within the profession.
The evidence against Mary Magdalene was incriminating, but Jesus was intent on illustrating that God is always ready and willing to forgive.

Forms of the word: incriminatory

Intrinsic

1. belonging to a thing by its very nature.

In the classic late 1960's film *Easy Rider,* Captain America possessed an intrinsic yearning to find the truth about himself - and so rode toward his demise.
Surely the need to ask ourselves questions as to the origin of our species is an intrinsic aspect of being human.
Fundamentally, we all possess an intrinsic free will that we can use to determine whether we are good people or bad people.

Forms of the word: intrinsically

Obtrusive

1. obtrude = to push oneself or itself forward, especially too much; intrude.

It would be a gross understatement to say that Donald Trump was obtrusive in the way he scrambled his way to the top in the fight for the Republican Party nomination.
It is an unfortunate fact of the corporate world but obtrusive people do disproportionately gain promotion ahead of people who are meek.
In their role of questioning of suspects, the CIA interrogators were habitually obtrusive.

Forms of the word: obtrusively

Paucity

1. smallness of quantity; fewness; scantiness.

Considering how many wealthy people there are in the world today there seems to be a dire paucity of philanthropists.
Prior to now, there has been an abysmal paucity of politicians willing to stand up to the timber industry for the sake of saving our forests.
The Academy was justifiably criticised for the paucity of African Americans nominated for awards.

Profound

1. having or showing great knowledge or deep understanding.

Former United States President Abraham Lincoln made one of the most profound decisions in human history, when he abolished slavery and gave rise to the civil war that eventually united this greatest of nations.
Albert Einstein had a profound understanding of the way that God had created the universe.

2. going beyond the surface; not superficial or obvious.

Do not enter the human services professions or careers unless you have a profound affinity for assisting people who are downtrodden.

Reprehensible

1. deserving to be rebuked; blameworthy.

It is totally reprehensible that successive governments have failed to install adequate earthquake and tsunami warning systems in the Pacific and Indian Oceans.
The present day attitudes of some young people towards elderly citizens, as an easy target for a quick theft, are so absolutely reprehensible.

The contrived activities of wealthy people and corporations to flout taxation laws through tax havens is reprehensible, as it moves the tax burden onto others.

Surreptitious

1. acting in a secret, stealthy way.

The international drug traffickers were constantly devising surreptitious ways of moving copious volumes of illicit drugs around the world, concealing compartments within complex machinery such as vehicle engines and within bulk food packaging.
Some people will endeavour to take more than their legal share of lobster from our oceans by one surreptitious means or another.
If intelligent extra-terrestrial beings have established bases here on Earth, be it beneath the oceans or deep within the Earth's crust, they are going about their activities in a very surreptitious manner.

Forms of the word: surreptitiously

Tantamount

1. equivalent, usually in value, force, effect, or meaning.

The activities of the corporate rich ruling class were branded by the new President as being tantamount to a legalistic form of expropriation of assets from middle class families.
Gross exploitation of non-renewable resources is virtually tantamount to robbing from our own children and future generations.
The invasion of the sovereign state of Kuwait by Iraqi forces was tantamount to an act of war.

Tenable

1. able to be held, supported, or defended, as against attack or objection.

It is quite tenable that with appropriate education programs people in both western and eastern countries will eventually subscribe to a range of views that embrace the belief systems of the other.
Sociologists would regard as quite tenable the idea of strengthening social bonds between our young people and senior citizens by interchange programs conducted through the school system.
Dr. Michio Kaku put forth the tenable proposition that intergalactic travel or time travel might be possible through wormholes in space-time.

Usurp

1. to take or make use of (rights, property, etc.) not one's own.

The Supreme Court decreed that this type of commercial activity was virtually a systematic usurpation of the assets of families, who made the mistake of thinking the shopping centre property developers were people of good repute.
There were no overt communications nor specific details pertaining to methods to be utilised in their pursuits, but a coincidence of interest ensured that many medical professions played a role in usurping as much of the federal budget as possible.
The large supermarket chains sell subsidised staple items such as milk and bread to usurp customers from the smaller chains.

Forms of the word: usurpation

Vagary

1. a wild, fanciful or fantastic action; freak.

The lives of so many innocent people had disintegrated as a mere vagary of the stock market.

With so many towns in mid-west United States obliterated every year by twisters, the lives of entire populations are subject to the vagaries of weather systems.

The vagaries of the legal system are such that most victims of corporate fraud will never receive justice or compensation.

Forms of the word: vagarious

Chapter 22

Compunction

1. uneasiness of conscience or feelings; contrition; remorse.

The instigators of propaganda to radicalise youth into acts of terrorism will feel absolutely no compunction about the subsequent mass murder of innocent civilians.
People involved in wilful, pre-meditated and systematic fraud to rob other people of their assets, do not normally suffer from any compunction about the total demise of their victims.
Those aliens do not seem to have any compunction about closing down our nuclear missile silos.

Consternation

1. amazement and dread causing a person to feel shock or fear.

Ever since the horrific tsunami of December 2004, the people of most south-east Asian countries feel considerable consternation whenever there is an earth tremor.
The incidence of suicide bombing in Iraq had reached such epidemic proportions that every-day life for its citizens was lived with constant feelings of consternation.
To disclose that aliens have arrived on Earth would cause mass consternation among people who believe in God.

Delirious

1. delirium = a wildly excited or emotional state.

The Japanese people were totally delirious to find that the American black widow had been found in Japan, as well as the Australian redback spider.

The scientific community was absolutely delirious to learn that string theory supported the hypothesis that black holes in the centre of galaxies are doorways to parallel universes.
The first images of the Hubble Deep Space Field showing thousands of galaxies in the deepest space, had astronomers the world over in a totally delirious state.

Educe

1. to draw forth or bring out; elicit; develop.

Whilst driving the vast distance across Australia's Nullarbor Plain, people in cars will increasingly wave at each other, because isolation will educe stronger social bonding between us.
If lawyers feel some ambivalence about working in a truly relevant legal environment, where people pay for legal advice only where legal advice - rather than legal information - is actually required, we may have to educe more ethical behaviour from them.
In view of current events, we need to ask how we can educe a vociferous and unequivocal condemnation of terrorist violence, from the world's Islamic leaders.

Forms of the word: educed, educing

Elucidate

1. to make (something) understandable or clear; explain.

The liquidators had all relevant financial records at their disposal, but requested the company directors to elucidate upon their submission that the insolvency was due to factors beyond their immediate control.
The controversial archaeologist was called upon by the society to elucidate on his theory that the ancient Egyptian pyramids were constructed by an astral traveller with a ginormous spaceship.

The psychic man assured listeners that his powers of prediction emanated from heaven and elucidated as to how people can develop such powers only through adherence to the universal law and to the Great Commandment of Jesus.

Forms of the word: elucidated, elucidation, elucidatory

Emulate

1. to try to equal or do better than.

We would all do well to emulate the qualities espoused by Jesus in his Sermon on the Mount.

2. to imitate (someone respected or admired).

Many young people endeavour to emulate others they regard as heroes - usually sports stars or entertainers.
People should not have children unless they are of a particular character that their children would want to emulate.

Forms of the word: emulated, emulating, emulation

Ethos

1. the basic spiritual character of a culture.

Australia's traditional Aboriginal people live with a particular ethos whereby they personally identify with a living entity from the world around them, such as an emu or kangaroo or even a gum tree.
It is difficult to comprehend how modernisation can possibly occur in socialist states without a considerable change of ethos brought about by a gradual exposure to the benefits of a western lifestyle.
The peculiar ethos that motivates transnational corporations to flout taxation laws surely emanates from complicit action between their lawyers and their accountants.

Exhort

1. **to urge, advise, or ask (someone) urgently**.

The newly elected Catholic Pontiff would exhort his College of Cardinals to abrogate the requirement of priestly celibacy, as an urgent priority.
A slightly miffed American tourist stood on the pier at New Zealand's Milford Sound, exhorting Asian tourists to visit the Grand Canyon.
The President of the United Nations made an impassioned speech, exhorting all national representatives to completely endorse the proposal to eradicate all petrol and diesel vehicles, as the only way to prevent absolute catastrophe caused by climate change.

Forms of the word: exhortation

Indolent

1. **tending to avoid work; lazy.**

The Golden Gate Bridge and the Sydney Harbor Bridge are iconic landmarks, but what would they cost to build today with so many comparatively indolent people in the work force?
The incursion of Australia's redback spider into Japan would not have happened if those Japanese agricultural control officials had not been so indolent when they were supposed to be watching for spiders on sea containers.
No doubt the former Soviet Union was beleaguered by a vast army of indolent bureaucrats, police, soldiers and politicians.

Forms of the word: indolence

Instil

1. **to inject slowly or by degrees into the mind or feelings; insinuate.**

In reducing the incidence of bankruptcy in our economy it may be necessary to instil a greater sense of civic responsibility into our financial institutions and implore them to provide case management of debtors.
Traversing the tracks of New Zealand's "Fiordland" can only serve to instil one with a sense of proportion of one's insignificant self.
Educationists need to be far more proactive in instilling students with values such as adherence to the universal law, compassion and forgiveness.

Forms of the word: instilled, instilling

Invidious

1. attracting hatred or envy.

The incoming President of the United States would find herself making the invidious decision as to whether or not her country would continue to be the world's policeman ... ah … policewoman!
The preacher staunchly responded that one should not place oneself in the invidious position of being in a nightclub, at the time of the second coming of Jesus Christ.

2. meant to excite ill will or resentment or give offence.

Despite legislative changes to end discrimination in club membership, many private golf clubs and turf clubs invidiously persist with blatant discrimination against women.

Forms of the word: invidiously

Judicious

1. discreet; prudent; well advised.

The United Nations issued a stern statement to all nations that countries harbouring terrorists would incur their collective wrath, as a totally judicious warning of what such nations could expect in retaliation.

In failing to kowtow to public demand to imprison all juvenile car thieves, the judge thought of himself as being quite judicious.
The Malaysian High Court judiciously sentenced the former Prime Minister to a long prison term for usurping hundreds of millions of dollars of his nation's wealth.

Mitigate

1. to moderate the severity of.

The young man had nearly been killed by line hopping seconds before a train arrived, but his lawyer attempted to mitigate his sentence by claiming the lad was running late for a job interview.
Successive French governments endeavoured to mitigate their culpability in detonating nuclear devices at Mururoa Atoll, with reference to a perceived threat from Russia.
The tendency of Japanese whalers to mitigate adverse publicity with reference to scientific research, will not save them from profound public enmity.

Forms of the word: mitigated, mitigating

Plausible

1. having an appearance of truth or reason.

The detection of gravitational waves meant it was now plausible that intergalactic space travel just might allow the human race to colonise the universe.
Australians proposed the very plausible explanation that the redback spider had made her way into Japan in her favourite hiding spot - beneath an Aussie muscle car that was imported from Australia by a Japanese billionaire.
NASA has put forth the plausible hypothesis that life could exist in oceans beneath ice covered moons of Jupiter, Saturn, Neptune and Uranus.

Forms of the word: plausibility

Predicated

1. to declare; proclaim (verb).

One cynical person in the audience had the audacity to request of the preacher on which scriptural verse he predicated his assertion “that all people who go to nightclubs are part of the devil's empire”.
Lawyers acting for the transnational corporations asserted that the proposed new international corporate wealth tax legislation was predicated on a restriction of free trade and spite for wealthy people.
The women’s president of the exclusive golf club stood to assert that the government’s anti-discrimination legislation was predicated on the principle that eligibility for membership could no longer be based on gender.

Retrospect

1. contemplation of the past; a survey of past time, events, etc.

In retrospect, we should have placed more stringent controls over the military build-up within Germany after WWI.
It is only in retrospect that we realise that many of our dynamic small business people were obliterated by the non-enforcement of laws that were meant to protect them.
Some people are so wise in retrospect, having the benefit of hindsight, but it is a vastly different story when you have to make an important decision, not knowing what the future holds.

Forms of the word: retrospection, retrospective

Supercilious

1. proudly contemptuous.

The blame for the recent election loss could also be attributed to one previous party leader whose rather supercilious manner had placed him out of touch with the electorate.

The chanteuse was prepared to revel in the knowledge that so many people admired her so immensely but she was far too hoity-toity, toffee-nosed, uppity and supercilious to condescend to meet any of her admirers.
One important protocol of meeting British royalty is that you never lay a hand on these supercilious superiors, as Australia's Molly Meldrum and former Prime Minister Paul Keating had done.

Forms of the word: superciliousness

Tacit

1. not openly expressed, but understood; implied or inferred.

Some NATO leaders did not overtly endorse the gulf war, for fear of retribution from extremists, but gave their tacit approval behind closed doors.
Though it was illegal for police officers to retain any contraband for themselves, the hierarchy gave subtle, tacit approval by virtue of its reluctance to adequately monitor whether its officers were doing so.
Members of the so-called property council never produced any written details regarding rent increases, but there was an abundance of tacit communication at the bar following each national conference.

Forms of the word: tacitly, taciturn

Veritable

1. being truly such; genuine or real.

There is now so much personal testimony from former military personnel who were sworn to fifty years of confidentiality that the incidence of genuine alien presence in our skies is entirely veritable.
The anthropology lecturer insisted that the student's assertion that the Maya civilisation of Central America was superior to all other indigenous races, was not veritable as it was purely a value judgement.

The incidence of shark sightings and shark attacks in Western Australia in recent years is veritable evidence that the web of life in the world's oceans is undergoing profound change.

Forms of the word: veritably

Vilify

1. to speak evil of; defame.

The military establishment would openly vilify any personnel who defied confidentiality to divulge that direct contact with aliens had been ongoing for several decades since the first detonation of a nuclear device.
The Japanese Emperor himself took time out to vehemently vilify the officers for allowing a tiger snake and a sergeant bull ant to crawl from a shipping container onto the wharf.
The question remains as to when the world's Islamic leaders will vilify anybody who murders in the name of Allah.

Forms of the word: vilified, vilifying

Chapter 23

Ambivalent

1. ambivalence = the presence in a person of opposite and conflicting feelings towards a person or object.

The discovery of frozen Velociraptor eggs beneath the Antarctic ice following a meltdown caused by a meteor impact, caused the scientific community to be quite ambivalent about whether or not the eggs should be incubated.
The incursion of Russian forces in to the Autonomous Republic of Crimea led to feelings of ambivalence among NATO's military chiefs, regarding their future course of action.

2. ambivalence = an uncertainty or ambiguity, especially due to an inability to make up one's mind.

Fidel Castro's younger brother, Raul, suffered no ambivalence in allowing the United States President Barak Obama into his country.

Forms of the word: ambivalence

Anecdotal

1. short account of an amusing or interesting event.

There was no smoking gun of weapons of mass destruction but there was an abundance of anecdotal evidence that Saddam Hussein had been planning something sinister with chemical weapons.
Despite the evidence in possession of the police indicating that the accused was involved in the bombing, the Director of Public Prosecutions decided to abort the case as most of the evidence was merely anecdotal.
The case against Elvis for his definitely sexy hip movements on stage during the Ed Sullivan show was better than anecdotal – it was all that screaming!

Arraign

1. to charge (someone) with faults; accuse.

The Malaysian government would severely arraign its former Prime Minister for his blatant embezzlement of public funds, but he would probably never spend time in jail.
The incident of the bombing of the Greenpeace vessel led the international community to universally arraign the French government for what was, essentially, an act of war in peacetime.
Jim Morrison was brought before the courts and arraigned for allegedly exposing himself on stage.

Forms of the word: arraignment

Circumvent

1. to get the better of by cleverness; outwit.

The United States military decided to enforce a permanent confidentiality clause in employment contracts, in order to circumvent future revelations by Dr. Steven Greer's Disclosure Project about the government's contact with aliens.

2. to go around; avoid.

One of the main problems with contemporary politics is that our politicians are prepared to circumvent critical issues of national significance, for the sake of their own electoral fortune.
The government decided to pay off the protagonist for justice in an attempt to circumvent similar action against the government by thousands of other victims of crime.

Forms of the word: circumvention

Constrain

1. to repress or restrain.

With so many hundreds of people wanting to be among the first to go to Mars, we will need to constrain them because we can take just four people this time.
The bombing of the Greenpeace vessel caused many people worldwide to call for a military response against the French but the former New Zealand Prime Minister himself sought to constrain such passions.
To preserve Antarctica from mining giants, we must constrain all forms of human activity on the continent.

Forms of the word: constrained, constraining, constraint

Construe

1. to deduce by construction or interpretation; infer.

In any walk of life, if you are listening to a person making promises or giving undertakings, be very careful as to how you construe what is said.
Defence Counsel for the mining lobby was brought before the Senate Committee to explain why he seemed to have deliberately misconstrued the submissions made by the Aboriginal elders about the sacred sites.
Gossip mongers will deliberately and impetuously misconstrue anything you might say about somebody else.

Degrade

1. to lower in character or quality; debase.

Let's face it good people - to elect Donald as the next United States President will seriously degrade the status of this most important office in the eyes of the international diplomatic community.
Churches are unanimously against pornography because, despite the needs of men and arguments pertaining to prevention of sex crimes, they believe that women should not degrade their status to be mere sex objects.

In what proved to be a profoundly degrading experience, the prince of Lilliput had become the subject of public ridicule following the release of private conversations with his concubine.

Forms of the word: degradation, degradable, degraded

Deplore

1. to feel or express deep grief for or about; regret deeply.

The world stood united to deplore the incursion of the so-called Islamic State into Syria.
The process of western rationalisation of religious veneration will probably lead us, as a community, to one day deplore all pre-existing forms of fundamentalist bigotry in favour of charity, tolerance and compassion.
Everybody admired Princess Diana for her works of charity and most of her admirers deplored the way she was ostracised by the Royal family when she decided to leave her husband.

Forms of the word: deplored, deploring, deplorable

Despise

1. to look down upon, as with hate or contempt; scorn; disdain.

Apart from the fact that the bombing of the Greenpeace vessel in peace time resulted in the murder of one man, this act of total cowardice caused other nations to despise the French for their typical arrogance.
Though Fidel Castro continued to despise the United States President, it was not lost on the Cuban population that Barak Obama is black - and the Castro family is white.
A true measure of character is the extent to which you despise any other person, without due reason.

Forms of the word: despised, despising, despicable, despicably

Digress

1. to wander away from the main subject in speaking or writing.

When delivering any type of verbal exposition it is so easy to digress then have difficulty remembering what it was that you were talking about.
The high school students had to be cautious about digressing when they were debating current events.
Before explaining that those aliens with skinny leathery bodies, large heads and big black almond-shaped eyes are actually us from our future, the President digressed, describing how we had evolved from the distant past and the small extremely bright planet the aliens had come from.

Forms of the word: digression, digressive

Ensconce

1. to settle comfortably or firmly.

Before sitting for your driving licence test, be sure to firmly ensconce the road rules within your mind.
Future generations of Libyan people must enjoy the expectation that a participatory democracy will be ensconced within their political landscape.
The concept of "let the buyer beware" may indeed be ensconced within common law, but that does not take precedence over any form of activity that is deemed illegal under specific legislation.

Forms of the word: ensconced, ensconcing

Espouse

1. to make (idea, cause, etc.) one's own; adopt; embrace.

The bishop appeared before the parliamentary inquiry into the sex industry to state that he and the church did espouse the view that men of reason could live without requiring any form of sexual gratification.

The Earl of Shaftsbury stood before the British Parliament in 1832 to petition that he espoused the belief that children should not be forced to work as chimney sweepers.
The vast majority of good Muslim people do, in fact, espouse the belief that terrorists are the infidel referred to in the holy Quran and deserve having jihad inflicted upon them.

Forms of the word: espoused, espousing

Evoke

1. to call up, or produce (memories, feelings, etc.).

Nothing will evoke sentiments and feelings as much as the photographs we preserve of our deceased loved ones.
Of all the actions of humans that evoke emotion more than any other, it is that adults expose children to the horrors of war and of genocide.
Few things will evoke more anger from citizens and businesses that need to borrow money, than the requirement to pay higher interest rates than wealthy people do.

Forms of the word: evoked, evoking, evocative

Flagrant

1. openly bad; glaring; notorious.

Bikie groups have become the most flagrant distributors of illicit drugs to young people.
The Spanish conquistadors were sent forth to colonise the New World and displayed flagrant hostility toward the indigenous Aztec and Inca people of Central and South America.
The so-called graffiti artists were caught on closed circuit television flagrantly defacing commercial billboards near the train line.

Forms of the word: flagrantly

Imminent

1. **likely to happen at any moment; impending.**

With the recent detection of gravitational waves it seems that the next major breakthrough in the metaphysical sciences pertaining to our understanding of the universe is imminent.
The time for the widespread circulation of basic information pertaining to legal issues that, until now, has been deemed as advice that can only be imparted by a lawyer, is imminent.
Perhaps these floods, drought, hurricanes and cyclones are a warning from nature that the advent of the next Ice Age is imminent.

Forms of the word: imminence

Implicit

1. **unquestioning, absolute.**

As citizens we are entitled to have implicit faith in our institution of law, but many legal professionals will bastardise it one way or another, for love of money.

2. **suggested, rather than actually stated.**

The whistleblower did not divulge that aliens had prevented us from self-destruction but implicit in his comment was that, being 'us' from our future, the aliens knew how climate change exterminated the bees – then the trees!

3. **contained in effect, although not in name or fact; inherent.**

Though it was not an explicit statement to exonerate the bungee jump operators for the tragedy, the judge ruled that bearing the risk was an implicit aspect of paying one's money for the ride.

Malaise

1. a vague feeling of bodily weakness or mental discomfort.

People who are afraid of flying usually experience feelings of malaise as the plane leaves the ground.
The tendency of Chinese manufacturers to usurp new products released via eBay causes malaise among most potential innovators.
The people of Queensland felt considerable malaise about yet another submission to mine the Great Barrier Reef.

Obtuse

1. insensitive or dull in awareness or feeling; stupid.

One American who had traversed the Grand Canyon several times made a totally obtuse remark to the tour guide that New Zealand's Milford Sound was an upside down version of his Grand Canyon.
People who get drawn in by peddlers of fanatical religious passion that is based on denigrating others' beliefs are prone to being rather obtuse people.
The Heaven's Gate sect who believed the Hale-Bopp Comet concealed a spaceship that would take them to another planet, were so obtuse as to be stupid beyond belief.

Repudiate

1. to refuse to recognize as having power or binding force.

The United Nations Security Council would stand resolute to repudiate the Russian claim to sovereignty over the Crimea.
Like so many dictators before him, the former Libyan President Muammar Gaddafi appeared on Libya's national television network to repudiate the counter movement and refute all allegations of corruption levelled against him.
Following the police insurgence into the Aboriginal community the state Premier endeavoured to repudiate its claim to land rights and refute that this

was an attempt to subjugate the Aboriginal people for the sake of the mining lobby.

Forms of the word: repudiated, repudiating, repudiation

Transgress

1. to pass over or go beyond (a limit, etc.).

The Chinese government had once again decided to transgress into the South China Sea by constructing an artificial island.
The bombing of the vessel in Auckland Harbor was obviously an act where the military of one nation sets out to transgress the sovereignty of another.
The Chinese government could be covertly building aircraft carriers in concealed shipbuilding yards in a blatant transgression of international protocols.

Chapter 24

Adjunct

1. something added to another thing.

The businesswoman was very successful but also had a flair for writing, so she wrote her popular romance novels as an adjunct to her business income.
The staff trainer was cognisant of the importance of active learning in inducting new staff - but was not as aware of the importance of reinforcement as an adjunct to this.
Now that we have saved so many lives with compulsory seat belts, perhaps speed limiters would be a worthy adjunct to the modern day motorcar.

Capitulate

1. to surrender without conditions, or on particular terms.

The Syrian army finally forced the terrorists in Palmyra to capitulate - by blowing up the entire town.
New Zealand's All Blacks rugby team had finally won two successive World Cup tournaments by forcing Australia's Wallaby pack to capitulate.
That terrifying All Black Haka was an attempt to force their opponents to capitulate before the game had even started.

Forms of the word: capitulated, capitulating, capitulation

Conducive

1. leading; contributive.

We need international protocols that are conducive to the ongoing preservation of all the fauna on the Antarctic continent.
Bungee jumping from a helicopter without wearing a parachute may not be conducive to living to see one's grandchildren walk down the aisle.

The Chinese government's embargo on open access to the internet is not conducive to its people having a real understanding of the world.

Disparage

1. to speak of or treat as of little value; depreciate; belittle.

Perhaps we ought not disparage our lawyers who are responsible for upholding our system of law in the courts, simply because they make so much money in the process.
Obtrusive staff who are always seeking promotion will forever be making comments to supervisors to disparage their fellow staff.
The Malaysian government was subjected to so many disparaging comments from the families of victims because it was blatantly concealing facts about the captain of Malaysian Airlines flight MH370.

Forms of the word: disparaged, disparaging, disparagement

Dispel

1. to drive off in various directions; scatter.

As a nation we must do everything conceivable to dispel perceptions that we are intolerant of the cultures of other nations.
Highly successful people who build empires of commercial activity from virtually nothing more than bright ideas, will dispel any doubts that the road to future wealth lies in nurturing imagination into tangible production.
It is imperative for the world's Islamic leaders to fervently and vehemently dispel all notions that endorse any forms of violence in the name of Islam.

Forms of the word: dispelled, dispelling

Duress

1. the use of threats or force.

It was only under considerable duress that the Malaysian government allowed foreign media into the courtroom following the air disaster.
It was under the duress of a possible international boycott of Chinese products that the Chinese government acceded to calls to purge pirates within its manufacturing sector.

2. the loss of freedom by force; imprisonment.

The entire free world is appalled at the duress inflicted upon all political dissenters in Vladimir Putin's Russia.

Encapsulate

1. to put in shortened form; condense; abridge.

The shrewd young student had such an aversion to reading the recommended voluminous novels that he, instead, merely read commentary he found on the internet, that encapsulate the meaning of the text books.
One woman who had been extremely successful in assisting other women into starting their own business ventures enounced her view that the publication should encapsulate the copious detail in taxation legislation.
Having powerful words at your fingertips will encapsulate and crystallise your thoughts.

Forms of the word: encapsulated, encapsulating

Impinge

1. to go beyond the proper limits; trespass; infringe.

There is a lot to be said for ensuring that you will be able to withstand the heat of competition if you impinge upon your competitor's trading ground.

Should we endeavour to abolish casinos when to do so would surely impinge upon a legitimate form of the government's revenue raising bases?
The business broker who was trying to procure a purchaser felt the business assessor's presence was an impingement upon his territory.

Forms of the word: impinged, impinging, impingement

Indignant

1. strong displeasure at something thought to be unworthy, unjust or wrong.

Who can blame Aboriginal people for becoming somewhat indignant when state governments and mining companies are in cahoots to undermine the rights bestowed upon them by the High Court?
Husbands and wives are likely to become extremely indignant if casino authorities refuse information about the habits of their spouse.
If you offer dubious service as a businessperson, you should expect some very indignant customers.

Forms of the word: indignantly

Inimitable

1. not able to be imitated, unique.

Elvis Presley's good looks, his voice, his demeanour and his movements were so inimitably Elvis, that all the imitators really do not even come close.
Many beautiful bird calls are seemingly inimitable, but don't tell that to Australia's lyrebird who can virtually imitate any sound.
The Beatles were perhaps even more inimitably unique than either Elvis or Michael Jackson.

Forms of the word: inimitability

Obdurate

1. **hardened against persuasion; hard-hearted.**

Fundamentalist Christian churches still cling so obdurately to their belief in Young Earth creationism, despite there being new evidence that man-like apes walked the Earth as long as seven million years ago.

2. **refusing to change one's ways.**

We know that politics and power is worth a lot of money, but why do our politicians need to be so obdurate in failing to eliminate fossil fuels.
The newly elected United States President excoriated Congress over its obduracy in failing to provide adequate health cover for the little people.

Forms of the word: obduracy, obdurateness

Ostensibly

1. **ostensible = outward; pretended; professed.**

The intransigence of the judges in avoiding mandatory sentencing for petty crimes was ostensibly from being judicious rather than pertaining to overcrowded prisons.
The entire thrust of affirmative action legislation was, ostensibly, to address inequality of opportunity for women attributable to various forms of career entrenchment and self-perpetuation.
Men in black coerced witnesses to the Roswell crash with threats of death, ostensibly for the purpose of national security.

Preside

1. **to occupy the place of authority or control.**

Of all the despicable acts of humanity there are few more repulsive than those of people who are supposed to preside over the carriage of justice, but who abrogate this expectation for the sake of their own wealth.

Why do successive governments preside over massive budget deficits when price control of commercial rents in the retail sector would create a flurry of commercial activity?
How much longer will the United Nations preside over the mass murder of millions of North Korean citizens by their own government?

Forms of the word: presided, presiding

Prevalent

1. widespread; in general use or acceptance.

They filmed *Lord of the Rings* in New Zealand because the abundance of mysterious looking geological landforms to conjure imagery of middle Earth is so prevalent in this beautiful land.
They filmed *Priscilla - Queen of the Desert* in outback Australia because the imagery of us macho bronzed Anzacs digging up gold in that bloody red dust in the Australian outback is so prevalent in the minds of people of other nations.
The formation of new galaxies and stars in the universe is so prevalent, that when we do colonise the universe, we will never deplete its resources.

Forms of the word: prevalence

Promulgate

1. to spread (a belief, teaching, etc.) widely among people.

Few people are as deplorable as extremists who promulgate sentiments against refugees who have been forced to flee their homeland.
Extreme groups from the left and from the right of politics are notorious for promulgating views that do not reflect the conventional opinions of the broader community.

As the Senate enquiry was preparing to sit the mining lobby was extremely active promulgating the concept of terra nullius, that Australia belonged to no-one prior to European settlement.

Forms of the word: promulgated, promulgating, promulgation

Proponent

1. someone who puts forward a proposal.

As the proponent of the concept of re-usable rockets Elon Musk addressed the NASA scientists on its viability.

2. someone who supports a cause.

American Bob Lazar became the main proponent of a plan for archaeologists to search for extra-terrestrial spacecraft that were buried beneath the Earth's surface.
She instigated a website to elicit views of the common people, as she was to be the proponent of a new middle of the road political party based on rectitude.

Purport

1. to say or claim.

Perhaps the most effective way for former socialist states to affect a transition to a free enterprise economy would be to sponsor people who purport to be able to mobilise imagination and materialise this into tangible outcomes.
If you purport to be a person of integrity you should ensure that your actions and behaviour reflect this.
Politics is beleaguered by people who purport to be community leaders but who usually have ulterior motives pertaining to money.

Respite

1. a delay or discontinuance for a time, especially of anything upsetting or trying; an interval of relief.

One ufology expert postulated that the aliens had been coming to Earth for a considerably long time seeking respite, because they had literally destroyed their own planet with global warming.
They had taken refuge under a boab tree to seek some respite from the searing desert sun.
There was no respite for alchemists during the Spanish Inquisition, as hundreds were burned at the stake.

Superfluous

1. being more than what is enough or needed; unnecessary.

The Qantas board decided to retrench one hundred executive staff that it regarded as superfluous to operations, which leads one to wonder why they were there in the first place.
With the advent of new technology typewriters, facsimiles and telephone landlines have become somewhat superfluous.
Perhaps a technology-based participatory democracy could render most of our politicians as superfluous!

Surmise

1. to think (something) without certain or strong evidence; conjecture; guess.

From the sudden disappearance of dinosaurs from the planet Earth about sixty-five million years ago and some anecdotal evidence, we can surmise that a catastrophic event took place that obliterated them.

With so many stars in our own Milky Way galaxy, it is preposterous not to surmise that there are numerous planets within the universe capable of supporting life as we know it.

From the ousting of dictators in north African and Middle Eastern nations and their move towards democratic rule, we can only surmise that the technology that is bringing the world closer together will ensure more of the same.

Forms of the word: surmised, surmising

Chapter 25

Allude

1. to speak of indirectly or casually.

When questioned about aliens by Jimmy Kimmel the United States President Mr. Barak Obama certainly did rather humorously allude to the aliens being in control.
Though he did not wish to rile the American tourists with comparisons between the Grand Canyon and Milford Sound, the tour guide alluded to the fact that Milford Sound is far more beautiful than the Grand Canyon.
Though the former Australian Liberal Party Prime Minister did not actually state that the man who held his baby above his head was a murderer, he certainly won an election by alluding to the same.

Forms of the word: alluded, alluding, allusion, allusive, allusively

Attenuate

1. to weaken or reduce in force, quantity or value.

Let us never attenuate our requirement that both lawyers and politicians be far more accountable for what they fail to do, more so than for what they actually do.
We should never attenuate our pursuit of values that are even more important than democracy - such as justice, equity, truth, loyalty and compassion.
Oppressive states such as North Korea and China will never attenuate their subjugation of citizens, until the free world puts a satellite in orbit above them that circumvents those nations' forbidding of free information.

Capricious

1. a tendency to change one's mind without apparent reason; whim.

In any typical workplace there will be capricious decision making by management that elevates less-worthy employees over more worthy employees.
The accusers of alchemists during the Spanish Inquisition were flagrantly capricious in making their accusations.
The astronauts planning their return trajectory to planet Earth had to be precise and avoid any capricious decision making.

Forms of the word: capriciousness

Corroborate

1. **to make more certain; confirm.**

The eccentric businessman created a new industry by offering substantial rewards to people who could corroborate allegations against big time swindlers.
A naturalist was flown in to corroborate that it was the Superb Lyrebird that was making noises like a construction gang in the forest, throughout the night.
Throughout the Spanish Inquisition there was no paucity of witnesses to corroborate that every accused person was, indeed, a witch.

Forms of the word: corroborated, corroborating, corroboration, corroborative

Derision

1. **the act of making fun of someone; ridicule; mockery.**

Voted as the most humorous film of the twentieth century, Monty Python's "Life of Brian" was a classic case of levelling derision at virtually every form of civil and civic reality – especially at the force-feeding of Latin to high school students.
As he stood accused before Pontius Pilate, Jesus was subjected to derisive taunts from the mob who sought his crucifixion.

People have been very derisive toward Sarah of Alaska - but with good reason.

Forms of the word: derisive, derisory

Detrimental

1. loss, damage, or physical hurt.

There is no doubt that the obduracy of the present day Israeli leadership towards the establishment of a Palestinian state has a detrimental effect on the peace process.
The recent upsurge in violence against the international community has had a detrimental effect on the travel industry.
It will be to the detriment of future generations that we exhaust the world's stocks of fish in the oceans.

Forms of the word: detriment, detrimentally

Immaterial

1. unimportant.

It was the example of one Good Shepherd, who had refused to leave even just one of his sheep out in the cold that compelled the justice campaigner to render all nefarious insurance companies as immaterial, by initiating a class action against them.
The judge regarded the defence argument that the alleged drug runners were under duress from drug barons who threatened to destroy their families, as immaterial.
If we continue to deplete the world's population of trees, all talk of future generations will be completely immaterial.

Impetus

1. a moving force; impulse; stimulus.

The impetus for such an extraordinary action as this litigation finance could be found in the way defence lawyers had allowed the situation to develop to the point that so many innocent victims of wrongdoing committed suicide.
The ongoing destruction of this one and only planet that we do have just might provide the impetus for NASA to find another one.
The impetus for future innovation will probably emanate from venture capital corporations.

Implore

1. to call upon (a person) in an urgent or humble manner, for help, mercy, etc.; beseech; entreat.

The group of corrective social workers made a united representation to implore the government to adopt the high-income subsidised employment plan for ex-offenders, so that they might break the cycle of crime.
This first President implored her people to follow her down a road of prosperity, equity, security, cooperation and peace.
Confucius preached his version of the universal law by imploring people to do nothing to others that they would not like done to themselves.

Forms of the word: implored, imploring

Impugn

1. to attack by words or arguments; challenge as false.

As the ocean yacht race had ended in total disaster with many people dead and others injured, the subsequent inquiry would undoubtedly impugn the weather forecasters.
Australia's first President was not averse to criticising the Parliament for its lack of action on critical social issues, so as to impugn both sides of the house.

The former Queen of England had impugned the insurance companies for being so tardy in compensating victims of the Christchurch earthquakes.

Forms of the word: impugnable

Obviate

1. to meet and get rid of or prevent (difficulties, objections, etc.) by effective measures.

The licensing requirement for people working in the forestry industry was an attempt by the government to obviate any future claim, by even more displaced persons, that their livelihood depended on the industry.
If we elect a person of immense rectitude as our President, we could obviate the need to increase the number of Members of Parliament.
The rapid expansion of ocean-based fish farming would obviate the need to degrade so much potential farming land.

Forms of the word: obviated, obviating, obviated

Pernicious

1. highly hurtful; ruinous.

As his way of retaining power, the young supreme leader of North Korea was following the footsteps of his pernicious father in ensuring that his generals and colonels were grossly over-remunerated.

2. deadly; fatal.

The airliner had been downed by the firing of a missile in a pernicious act by Russian military personnel.

3. evil or wicked.

So now the entire world is waking up to the fact that if we do not act with haste to curtail the activities of pernicious terrorists before they gain any stronghold, it will cost us even more to eradicate them.

Pertinent

1. relating to the matter in hand; relevant; apposite.

Despite the best efforts of the renegade dictator to conceal his weapons, the United Nations weapons inspectors were able to determine that there had been weapons production by focusing on the pertinent questions pertaining to the importation of dangerous chemicals.
In a new global economy one of the most pertinent reasons for governments not gaining an unfair advantage for their own people by subsidising export products, will be the unilateral retaliation by the remainder of the market.
True to form, the Russian President denied that his country had brought down the passenger jet by levelling blame at rebels, but the International Court of Justice focused on the pertinent facts.

Forms of the word: pertinence

Pragmatic

1. treating historical events with special reference to their causes and results.

The United Nations weapons inspectors were sufficiently pragmatic to know that the dictator's nuclear arsenal was buried beneath his own prince's palaces.
In determining their future directions, Australia's indigenous people will need a pragmatic approach to ensure they are no longer exploited.
The New Zealand government had no choice but to pragmatically declare some entire suburbs of Christchurch as uninhabitable.

Forms of the word: pragmatical, pragmatically, pragmatism, pragmatist

Rectitude

1. rightness of principle or practice.

Nothing was going to deter this President of immense rectitude from delivering to the people exactly what they expected of their political system.
The philanthropists were genuinely people of rectitude in providing the funds to construct the Three Gorges Dam.
We Australians have sufficient rectitude to ensure that we will not be deterred from living up to our international responsibilities toward refugees, by a few bad apples.

Regress

1. to move in a backward direction; go back.

The real problem with so many convicted criminals who re-offend is that without appropriate programs offering rehabilitation they will regress into more serious crime.
The physical evolution of the human species has taken place over millions of years, but there has been nothing regressive about it.
The exhortations of Donald Trump to ban Muslim people from entering the United States were duly branded by all former Presidents as regressive.

Forms of the word: regression, regressive, regressively

Retract

1. to withdraw (a statement, opinion, promise etc.).

Despite some cursory attempts by the law society to allow its members to make contingency arrangements, the fledgling lawyer refused to retract his own "no win – no fee" service.
This Australian President of the people had made it clear to the Parliament that she was not averse to retracting the charter of the Parliament and send the politicians back to the people.

Leonardo Da Vinci was forced to retract his statements pertaining to the solar system, by church cardinals, who knew nothing at all about science.

Forms of the word: retractable, retraction

Subterfuge

1. something, as a plan, trick, etc., used to hide or avoid something or to escape an argument.

The law society then accused the litigation financier, who was actually a person of considerable rectitude, of implementing a particularly nasty form of subterfuge for the purpose of creating her own wealth.
The autocratic dictator resorted to subterfuge in trying to deflect the United Nations inspectors, by concealing weapons of mass destruction in vast underground bunkers.
The Liberal Party of Australia has won a number of federal and state elections by one form of subterfuge or another.

Transpose

1. to cause (two or more things) to change places; interchange.

The litigation financier had utilised his acumen to transpose the horrendous cost of litigation from the victims back onto the wrongdoers.
The people had managed to transpose power away from politicians and to return it to where the forefathers of democracy, Jean Jacques Rousseau and John Stuart Mill, had always intended for it to preside - with the people.
Through progressive increases in their scheduled fees, the legal fraternity had managed to transpose its taxation liability back onto the consumer.

Forms of the word: transposed, transposing, transposition

Volition

1. the act or power of willing.

The young missionaries undertook to go overseas, knocking on doors to convert the heathen, of their own volition - except that they had better if they want to subsequently be offered a job in Salt Lake City.
None of the medical staff had been coerced into spending time in Africa among the homeless children - it was of their own volition that they had volunteered for this humanitarian mission.
In the end, whether you choose to be a good person or not, is entirely a question of your own volition.

www.ingramcontent.com/pod-product-compliance
Lightning Source LLC
LaVergne TN
LVHW050623100826
845148LV00011B/1707

* 9 7 8 0 9 7 5 0 9 9 8 5 8 *